THE GOSPEL ACCORDING TO ST. MARK

NEW TESTAMENT FOR SPIRITUAL READING

VOLUME 3

Edited by

John L. McKenzie, S.J.

THE GOSPEL
ACCORDING TO ST. MARK

Volume I

RUDOLF SCHNACKENBURG

CROSSROAD • NEW YORK

1981
The Crossroad Publishing Company
575 Lexington Avenue, New York, NY 10022

Originally published as *Das Evangelium nach Markus 1*
© 1966 by Patmos-Verlag
from the series *Geistliche Schriftlesung*
edited by Wolfgang Trilling
with Karl Hermann Schelke and Heinz Schürmann

English translation © 1971 by Sheed and Ward, Ltd.
Translated by Werner Kruppa

Library of Congress Catalog Card Number: 81-68165
ISBN: 0-8245-0112-8

PREFACE

The Fathers of the Church wrote lengthy commentaries on all the books of the Bible, both Old and New Testaments. The collection of these commentaries runs into tens of thousands of pages. Interest in the Bible obviously was wide and deep; and it is surprising that commentaries on the Gospel of Mark are very few in the period of the Fathers of the Church, and no commentary on Mark was written by those who are regarded as the major Fathers. The Fathers thought rather poorly of Mark; Augustine said that Mark was simply an abbreviation of Matthew. The Fathers observed something which close reading reveals, that Mark is contained almost entirely in Matthew and Luke. These Gospels, like John, are rich just where Mark seems impoverished, in the sayings of Jesus. Mark often says that Jesus taught, but he rarely tells what it was that Jesus taught. Hence whatever of value Mark had would be found in the other Gospels; and there was nothing of Mark's own that deserved attention.

Modern criticism places Mark as the first of the Gospels, and hence Mark has an interest which the other Gospels lack; it is precisely what the Fathers did not think it was, an original work. It is Matthew and Luke who are the large-scale borrowers, and the scope of their Gospels can be seen by studying how they use the material which they take from Mark. In this commentary Mark is called " the young church's book of faith "; it is as close as we can come to the original response of faith to Jesus the Risen Lord. This does not mean that Mark is, so to speak, pure faith without any theological interpretation; it does mean that we cannot compare Mark to his sources as we can compare Matthew and Luke to Mark.

The Gospel of Mark can perhaps be most easily understood if it is seen that it announces Jesus as an event and not as a teacher. The description is not beyond misunderstanding; the other three Gospels do not lose sight of Jesus as an event when they become much more explicit about Jesus as teacher and about his doctrine. In Mark Jesus is commonly addressed as " Teacher," the title which in Judaism appears as rabbi. The rabbi was a student and teacher of the Law and its traditional interpretations. He gathered about himself a group of disciples who would preserve his teaching and in their turn expand it. The rabbis and their disciples thought of themselves as living in the stream of tradition to which they contributed. Evidently Jesus looked like a rabbi and was regarded as a rabbi. It was the purpose of Mark to show that he was much more; and to designate this " much more " we have chosen the term " event."

The event is the saving event expected in Judaism. The belief was formed on the basis of a number of Old Testament texts, but in Judaism it received a definiteness of form which it did not have in the Old Testament. As associated with a saviour figure called the Messiah, the event was expected to be the saving act of God which would restore the dynasty of David and the empire of Israel. It does not appear that this was realistically expected throughout Judaism. The Pharisees saw the fulfillment of Judaism in life under the Law; the Sadducees saw the fulfillment in the worship of the one true God in his temple. The messianic expectation had strong political and secular coloring more often than not.

The faith of the young church professed that the saving act of

God had occurred in Jesus without conquest and empire, without the Law, without the temple and sacrifice. In fact the young church announced that the saving act of God ended the validity of such sacred institutions as Law and temple, and denied that the reign of God had any association with the political ambitions of Israel. The proclamation of the saving act as accomplished in the death of Jesus on the cross and his resurrection from the dead was, in the words of Paul, scandal to the Jews and folly to the Gentiles. We have some difficulty in understanding the incredibility of the gospel proclamation to Jews and Gentiles. We are familiar enough with modern incredulity, but we do not readily see that the ancient world had its own forms of unbelief.

In presenting Jesus as an event, Mark intended to represent God as entering the world in Jesus; the phrase is used without any implications of incarnational theology which appears in later books of the New Testament. The world lies under the reign of Satan; this is not only the reign of sin, but the world in which man suffers the effects of sin. Among these effects are disease and death. In Jesus the reign of God appears in power. The power is the power to save and ultimately to deliver man from the reign of Satan. Disease is frequently—not always—associated with demonic power in Mark; the association is most easily made in diseases of which the ancient world knew neither the cause nor the cure. Whenever Jesus delivers a sufferer from illness, the power of Satan is pushed back and the reign of God advances. The association between healing and forgiveness of sin is made, again not always; but the implicit association is always there. As man is freed from sin, a door to freedom from the effects of sin is opened to him. The power of the Son of Man to heal is evidence of a far greater power to perform the real saving act, to release from sin.

Mark makes no effort to rationalize the paradox of the redeeming death. This is the way it must happen; the young church believed that it found this necessity in the scriptures, and it credited Jesus himself with this interpretation. The mystery of death becomes tolerable only in the light of the resurrection. The saving act is not accomplished by human might but by the power of God; and Paul said that power reaches its fullness in weakness.

Is not Mark's presentation of the victory of the reign of God over the reign of Satan mythological? Certainly it is; one should not conclude that it is therefore unreal. The gospel was proclaimed among peoples who thought mythologically, whether Jews or Gentiles. The event which was realized in Jesus was suprahistorical and transcendent of human experience. Mark presented the reality of the event in the terms best known to him and to those who heard the gospel. Mark did not attempt to make the gospel more credible by reducing its reality to the level of mere historical experience. To take a common example: when Caesar crossed the Rubicon, he was himself dimly aware of the incalculable consequences of his decision—but only dimly. The event itself, however, was something which occurs daily; its importance did not lie in what could be seen. So the event of Jesus was not only important but unique; neither did its dimensions lie in what was perceptible to eyes and ears and touch. The event was not only unique but enduring. Mark was the earliest Christian writer to attempt to present this reality in its full dimensions. The presentation was simple, because it was the vision of a simple man speaking to simple men. The learned man may be one of those to whom it is hidden while it is revealed to the simple.

JOHN L. McKENZIE

OUTLINE

THE MISSION OF THE TWELVE, ATTEMPTS TO WITHDRAW AND WAN-
DERINGS, GROWING MISUNDERSTANDING (6 : 6b—8 : 30)

I. The mission of the disciples and their return, the miracle of
the loaves and the walk on the water, further activity among
the people (6 : 6b–56)

II. Jesus disassociates himself from the false, precept piety of
the Jews (7 : 1–23)

III. Journeys into pagan territory, growing misunderstanding,
the balance of the Galilean ministry (7 : 24—8 : 30)

JESUS IS INVESTED WITH HIS OFFICE
AS SAVIOUR (1:1-13)

The Caption (1:1)

¹The beginning of the gospel of Jesus Christ.

The word " gospel " aptly expresses the contents and essence of
the teaching of Jesus. It is the news which he brings from God
in the time of fulfillment (1:15), the " good " news of God's
final will to rescue.

For the young church Jesus the proclaimer became the subject
proclaimed; the messenger of the gospel became its most prominent subject and content. Jesus *Christ*, the *Son of God* (as is
added in several manuscripts), is the center of the gospel as the
young church understands it in its Easter faith.

John the Baptist:
The Promised Precursor, the Voice in the Wilderness,
the Baptizer and Proclaimer of the Messiah (1:2-8)

²As it is written in Isaiah the prophet, " Behold, I send my mes-
senger before thy face, who shall prepare thy way; ³the voice of
one crying in the wilderness: Prepare the way of the Lord, make
his paths straight." ⁴John the baptizer appeared in the wilderness,
proclaiming a baptism of repentance for the forgiveness of sins.

3

⁵And there went out to him all the country of Judea, and all the people of Jerusalem; and they were baptized by him in the river Jordan, confessing their sins. ⁶Now John was clothed with camel's hair, and had a leather girdle around his waist, and ate locusts and wild honey. ⁷And he proclaimed saying, "After me comes he who is mightier than I, the thong of whose sandals I am not worthy to stoop down and untie. ⁸I have baptized you with water; but he will baptize you with the Holy Spirit."

The time of salvation dawning with Jesus already begins with the appearance of John the Baptist. This great preacher of repentance and preparer of the way belongs in the gospel, as Mark sees it, and not outside it as the last prophet before the new age, because in him the prophetic pronouncements are already being fulfilled. The double quotation of verses 2–3 (Mal. 3 : 1; Is. 40 : 3) combined under the uniform title of Isaiah, the prophet of salvation, conveys to the mind of the early Christians John's essential functions as they then appear in the narrative account (vv. 4–8). The baptizer in the Jordan is seen wholly with Christian eyes and is taken into the service of Jesus, the Messianic baptizer with the Holy Spirit, an instructive chapter on the early Christians' use of scripture and interpretation of history. The " Lord," which in Isaiah (and originally also in John) referred to God himself, who will come to his people on a broad and straight royal path as the saviour and ruler at the final time, is now Jesus, for whom the voice in the wilderness prepares the way. God's salvation, God himself, has come to us in Jesus.

Corresponding to the word of God for the final time, John the Baptist appears in the *wilderness*. Geographically, we are here concerned with the lower valley of the Jordan, not far from Jericho and the estuary of the river into the Dead Sea; but the expression has a religious significance here. As it is usually used in Mark, the word "wilderness" does not primarily mean the place where one flees to from the world to do penance, but rather the place of God's nearness (cf. 1:13) to which one, indeed, must "go out" to seek God, away from the hustle and bustle of men and the noise of cities. There John appears as a proclaimer ("herald"), a word which is also used for Jesus' activity (1:14, 38 and other places), and one should not allow the cheerful tone of this word to be dimmed by the words "baptism of penance." For what we usually translate as "penance" is rather *conversion* to God, a turning to the spring of life and beginning of true joy, the first response to God's good news of salvation (1:15). The "forgiveness of sins," however, is the beginning of salvation, of peace and association with God.

The voice of the Baptist finds a strong response. That the entire country of Judea sets out to him and *all* the people from Jerusalem is a promising sign. Through the mouth of the one crying in the wilderness God collects the people to whom Jesus then preaches the good news of salvation and from whom he can form his community. The people called allow themselves to be *baptized*, to be immersed by the Baptist in the Jordan, to be placed under God's judgment seat of grace by confessing their sins—a unique and special rite to escape the wrathful judgment of God and to belong to the community of God at the final time. John's baptism is only a preparation, but it nonetheless prefigures Christian baptism, which one must undergo just as willingly and obediently in order to achieve forgiveness and deliverance and become a member of Christ's salvation community. With his baptism, too, John prepares the way, fulfills a divine commission which he does not yet understand in its deeper meaning. His call to conversion, whose sign is baptism, has deeper echoes and becomes a challenge to be converted to the faith, to follow Jesus and join his community.

The seriousness of this moment in the history of salvation is emphasized by the prophetic figure and way of life of John. His nourishment and clothing are those of a dweller in the wilderness, scant and austere, and thus he admonishes the renunciation of earthly goods in order to be wholly free for God. But this ascetic trait is not the main thing; rather, John embodies for Mark the promised Elijah to which the quotation Malachi 3:1 (above, v. 2) refers, according to a Jewish interpretation of the text (cf. Sir. 48:10; Mal. 3:23).

The description of the Baptist's clothing is similar to those of Elijah. The old man of God wore " a garment of hair-cloth " and a " girdle of leather " (4 Kings 1:8); John is clothed with a rough garment made of camel's hair—unlike men of the world who wear soft, splendid clothes (cf. Mt. 11:8), and he too possesses only a " leather girdle," not an ornamental one as was usual with the rich (for their " pocket money "). His simple diet completes the picture of frugality which he presents to the businessmen and the soldiers, the rich citizens of Jerusalem and the poor farmers who pass along the way. *God is his portion, God's mission his strength.* The young church has underlined the Elijah tradition still further by combining John's place of baptism (on the eastern shore of the Jordan) with Elijah's place of departure: she built on the hill a church to Elijah, at the foot of which she honored the cave of the Baptist. Elijah, of whom we are reminded by other accounts from the ministry of Jesus, and John, who takes up his image and fulfills it, belong together: men of God, of austere piety, figures called by God into the history of salvation, witnesses to Christ from the distance of the Old Testament and from the imminence of Christ's arrival.

John, however, fulfills his actual vocation by *proclaiming the mightier one* who is coming after him. There is no doubt he means the Messiah. From what we know from the other two synoptists he imagined him above all as the executor of God's justice (cf. Mt. 3:7-10). Mark, however, understands this " mightier one " as the bringer of salvation who makes actual what the Baptist at the Jordan could only prepare for: " baptism with the Holy Spirit." Thus, for him, John becomes the " herald " of the Messiah; again the evangelist uses the cheerful word " proclaimed." The greatness of him who is coming, with his saving gifts and powers from God, is illustrated in the precursor by his unworthiness and smallness: he does not even find himself worthy of a servant's task—to untie the thong of his sandals whereby one must stoop down low. These are not servile, but manly words which express his reverence for the mightier one. The yardstick whereby he measures himself and the one coming after him is the work with which God has commissioned him and the Other and in which he partakes. He has only baptized with water and his baptism was only a preparation for the Messianic event, preparing the people of God; the " mightier one " will baptize with the Holy Spirit.

The *Holy Spirit* is the gift of the final time which will—quite differently from the waters of the Jordan—purify, sanctify and bind men to God in a lasting community as the prophet Ezekiel had foretold: " I will sprinkle clean water upon you and you shall be clean . . . A new heart I will give you, and a new spirit I will put within you, and cause you to walk in my statutes . . . You shall be my people and I shall be your God " (Ezek. 36:25-29). Such thoughts, which were also prevalent in the

Qumran community, will have inspired the Baptist in his expectation of salvation. He believes that the one he is proclaiming
will possess, administer, and impart this power of the divine
Spirit. The evangelist and the Christian reader may also have
had that baptism in mind which they themselves received and
in which they experienced God's Spirit.

The Baptism of Jesus: Jesus of Nazareth,
Messiah and Son of God (1:9–11)

*⁹In those days Jesus came from Nazareth of Galilee and was
baptized by John in the Jordan. ¹⁰And when he came up out of
the water, immediately he saw the heavens opened and the Spirit
descending upon him like a dove; ¹¹and a voice came from
heaven, " Thou art my beloved Son; with thee I am well
pleased."*

A veil of mystery still lies over the person proclaimed by John;
then the name *Jesus of Nazareth* is heard, and soon there is no
longer any doubt; it is he. God himself acknowledges him. The
purpose of this concise account is not to describe the consecra-
tion of Jesus to Messiahship or even to explain the formation of
his Messianic consciousness; it is, rather, to make public that
Jesus is the promised Messiah, the baptizer with the Spirit, and
to indicate that the beginning of his ministry is animated by the
Spirit. It is irrelevant who at that time heard the voice of God
(not till the gospel of John does the Baptist " bear witness " to
the people, Jn. 1:32ff.); it is enough that the reader knows:
God acknowledges this Jesus as his anointed One. Mark relates
the event which occurs in connection with the baptism of Jesus

as it is experienced by Jesus: *he* saw the heavens open and the Spirit coming upon him, and God speaks to him: " *Thou* art my beloved Son . . ." But that is not meant to be an " experience " of Jesus; it is a divine revelation. As with the account of John the Baptist, it is news of God's salvation, and it becomes the mystery of Jesus proclaimed by the young church: he is the beloved Son of God anointed with the Holy Spirit.

The first sentence serves only as an introduction. What follows, the scene after the baptism of Jesus, is the proclamatory nucleus of the account. Because they are inessential, the exact circumstances are not mentioned. Only the fact that Jesus " came " from Nazareth to Galilee (from far away; previously only Jerusalem and Judea were mentioned) and " was baptized " is important. Jesus is identified by his home town as a definite historically existing man; he is no mythical figure. And over this (" historical ") Jesus there are then uttered these unprecedented words by the voice of God. It is the clear confession of the young church: this historical Jesus is *God's beloved, only Son.* All other considerations, such as why he subjected himself to the " baptism of repentance and forgiveness of sin," remain remote (different in Mt. 3:14f.). Only in the " going down into the Jordan " and " coming up out of the water " can one find perhaps a hint of a deeper understanding: he who humbly and obediently bowed his head under the hand of the Baptist, and subjected himself to the baptism of the entire people experiences a divine attestation. Serving without question, although already called to reign, he receives the seal of his Messianic office from God.

The scene of the revelation itself is portrayed in the symbolic language of the Old Testament. The *opening of the heavens* can signify that God is coming out of his transcendence as it occurs when the prophet receives a revelation (Ezek. 1 : 1); or, more aptly : the merciful condescension of God to proclaim again peace and salvation to humanity (cf. Lk. 2 : 13ff.). But the expression " the heavens were rent " points more closely to the sigh of longing for God's coming as in Isaiah 63 : 19: " O that thou wouldst rend the heavens and come down . . .!" This coming down of God is now accomplished in the manner of the *Spirit* descending on Jesus. It is at the same time a sign for the *anointed one as such*, the Messiah who is to possess the Spirit of God in fullness (Is. 11 : 2; 61 : 1).

The *voice from heaven* is the voice of God himself, hence not merely a *Bath Quol* (" the daughter of the voice "), as the Jewish doctors of the law conceived the imparting of revelation out of respect for God's transcendence. God addresses himself immediately to the one marked by and filled with the Holy Spirit: " You are my Son." In Psalm 2 : 7 God speaks thus to the King of Israel and accepts him as a son. But the connection with this " formula of adoption " becomes questionable when one compares the words which follow: " beloved," " with thee I am well pleased." For, they remind one of the words addressed to the " servant of God ": " Behold my servant, my chosen one, in whom my soul delights " (Is. 42 : 1), especially since to this is added: " I have put my Spirit upon him." Why then " my Son " and not " my servant "? Is this another translation of the Greek word *pais* which can mean both " child " and " servant "? But it is hardly a chance alteration; it is, rather, a conscious Christian interpretation. Jesus is both: that " chosen servant," since he obediently fulfills God's commission from his baptism to his death of atonement " for many " (cf. 10 : 45); at the same time, however, he is the only beloved Son (cf. 12 : 6), to whom God bears witness also at the transfiguration on the mountain

(9:7). Thus, "beloved" will have been intentionally substituted for "chosen."

Jesus in the Wilderness and the Temptation of Jesus: Preparation for Messianic Activity (1:12–13)

[12]The Spirit immediately drove him into the wilderness. [13]And he was in the wilderness forty days, tempted by Satan; and he was with the wild beasts; and the angels ministered to him.

With a dynamic "immediately," which is a characteristic of his style, Mark combines the story of the temptation with the event of baptism. *The Spirit* which has just descended on Jesus drives him out into the wilderness. With, as it were, an irresistible force he leads him into solitude, far away from men and alone with God. The temptation by Satan is not mentioned as the purpose of this abduction (as in Matthew). It occurs only on the occasion of his sojourn in the wilderness, but it probably extends through the entire period of the "forty days." If one considers the information, peculiar to Mark, that "he was with the wild beasts," the sojourn in the wilderness seems to have a more far-reaching significance in Mark than in the other synoptists. The temptation by Satan is not the only important event; the sojourn in the wilderness, the being together with the animals, and the ministering of the angels are noted as of equal significance. Nevertheless, the "temptation" is an inseparable part of this quiet period and puts its stamp on it. The succession of concise sentences indicates that all of Satan's efforts were fruitless and that the one driven out by the Spirit whom Satan pursued remained in peace and in communion with God.

The "wilderness" is a *place of decision*. Just as Israel was tempted in the wilderness, so the Anointed by the Spirit is tempted there by Satan. Israel, however, gave in to the temptation, whereas the " servant of God," representative too of the old people of God, God's beloved Son, was the victor. The number *forty* is a sacred number of the Bible: Israel was tested forty years in the wilderness (Deut. 8:2f., 15f.); Moses remained forty days and nights on the mountain (Ex. 24:18) where he prayed and fasted (Ex. 24:28); strengthened by nourishment given him by God, Elijah wandered forty days and nights to the mountain of God, Horeb (3 Kings 19:18). Mark does not say what the testing of Jesus consisted of, what Satan inspired him with and what he was tempting him to do. The fact alone is of sufficient importance: Jesus will feel the opposition of the powers of evil later, in his public ministry (cf. 3:22–27), but he will break it with the authority granted him (1:27), even though never independently of his union with his Father (cf. 14:36). The persistent temptations of Satan, the opponent of God and the anti-divine sovereign (3:23, 26), during that period in the wilderness, temptations which foreshadow the future, are surely directed against the Messiah and the work of salvation with which he is commissioned. They fail, however, because the bringer of salvation remains united with God, filled with the Spirit, and faithful to his mission.

Jesus was *with the wild beasts*. Is this intended to convey the power and victory of God's warrior over wild and unruly forces? In connection with the ministering angels, one is reminded of Psalm 91 (90):11ff.: the angels guard him who dwells under the protection of the Most High: " You will tread on the lion and the adder, the young lion and the serpent you will trample under foot." But the Greek turn of phrase more readily expresses a community with the animals, and the " ministration " of the angels (not noted till the end) refers, rather, to the offering of food and drink (cf. 3 Kings 19:5ff.). One ought not to imagine that Satan has taken charge of the wild animals and put them into the service of his pernicious ends, and to look on it merely as an environmental description for the wilderness and its terrible loneliness would be to miss the point of this meaningful account. More is at stake here: the Messiah who lives in communion with God also finds peace with animals dangerous to man. Psalm 91 may well have found an echo here, though not in the sense of a victory over the " wicked " animals, but rather in the sense of a reconciliation with God's creation. The thought of a " second Adam," who restores the age of paradise, does not occur anywhere else in Mark's gospel; but the friendliness of animals was expected for the Messianic era (Is. 11:6f.), and the Messiah filled with the divine Spirit (Is. 11:2ff.) experiences in his combat with Satan the fulfillment of that promise.

Finally, it is *God's messengers* themselves, the angels who *minister* to him. Just as after the fast of Jesus and the temptation of Satan we read in Matthew that " angels came and ministered to him " (Mt. 4:11) after God was challenged to produce nourishment, so Mark will also have had a strengthening with food and drink in mind. God will not allow his Messiah to starve and perish; the Father guarantees what is necessary for life. The angels are also a contrasting image of Satan, who seeks ruin and death; the good spirits contrast with the angel of darkness who has broken away from God. God's protection and providence, which is revealed in this scene, is, indeed, meant for the chosen one, the beloved who is to accomplish the work of salvation; but the scene will also be a promise to those who will follow in Jesus' footsteps.

PART I

THE GOOD NEWS OF SALVATION
(1:14—8:30)

INTRODUCTION

What the evangelist has so far recorded and proclaimed already belongs to the " gospel " as God's good news of salvation since it describes the dawn of the time of salvation in the appearance of John the Baptist and the introduction of Jesus into his office as Saviour. It is, nevertheless, only an introduction to the appearance of Jesus himself, to his preaching, teaching, his ministry in mighty deeds, his battle against opposing forces, and the gathering of a community of disciples. The opening of this main exposition is marked by the programmatic sentences in 1 : 14f. : now Jesus begins to proclaim the " gospel of God," whose main content is given in the words that follow. But how is one to understand the more detailed presentation and divisions in the long chapters up to the passion? Is it the aim of the evangelist to trace faithfully the course of Jesus' ministry? Should one take note of the geographical data which he gives and the course of his reports (chronological details are almost entirely absent up to 14 : 1), and attempt a division accordingly? Roughly the following sections would be the result:

I. The great Galilean ministry of Jesus (1 : 14—6 : 6ᵃ).

II. Jesus moves from place to place and into pagan territory (6 : 6ᵇ—10 : 45).

III. The journey of Jesus to Jerusalem and his final activity there (10 : 46—13 : 37).

IV. The passion and resurrection (14 : 1—16 : 8).

17

We do not deny that the evangelist has a certain interest in external facts such as place names. Yet if one takes note of certain self-contained sections coming more under systematic-theological considerations, one realizes that this is not the most prominent intention of the evangelist. The " conflict stories " in 2 : 1—3 : 6, at the end of which we already read that his opponents intend to destroy him (3 : 6); the chapter on the parables (4 : 1–34); the talk (7 : 1–23) which deals with a new type of inner piety and purity; the great instructions (10 : 1–45); the disputes in Jerusalem (11 : 27—12 : 44); the eschatological talk in chapter 13 : in a body these testify to a more didactic interest directed towards the community. The " geographical-historical " line is again and again interrupted by quite other viewpoints, and one must accept that the framework of the accounts is for the most part merely external and incidental. In reality the evangelist is concerned with illuminating the church of his time with what is lastingly valid, with what the church can and ought to learn from the ministry of Jesus in word and deed. Mark seems to present most of the material in " lessons " which, indeed, have an historical basis in Jesus' activity, but they do not rigidly follow the course of history. Rather, they are consciously composed from what Jesus said and did. Adapting ourselves to the view of the evangelist, the text will be disclosed with greater vitality to us in our situation as listeners than if we read it as an historical-biographical report. Hence it is useful to attempt a division corresponding to this viewpoint.

A pivotal point for the ministry of Jesus is probably given in 8 : 31 where Jesus begins to reveal to his disciples his way of suffering and death. The preceding Caesarea-Philippi scene (8 : 27–30) comes across as a kind of stock-taking of his public ministry up to that time : he had tried to win over the people to his message but the people did not understand the meaning of his message or what happened in his ministry ("the mystery of God's kingdom," 4:11) or, put in another way, they did not grasp the mystery of his person. Faced with this situation of misunderstanding and disbelief, he must then go the way of the cross and beyond the cross to glory in accordance with God's dispensation in order to realize his plan for salvation. That is how the evangelist sees it, and with his presentation he gives the communities a basis for their confession of Jesus, the Messiah who was crucified and rose again and as exalted has become the Saviour and Lord of all who join his community in faith. For that reason the evangelist already has the later church in mind whose foundation he can recognize in the earthly ministry of Jesus and for whom he wishes to disclose what in the teaching and activity of Jesus is meaningful to her. The "ecclesial" concern of the evangelist is evident in part one in the sections which refer to the circle of disciples and are inserted into this section like landmarks:

1. The call of the disciples (1:16–20).
2. The election of the twelve (3:13–19).
3. The mission of the twelve (6:6ᵇ–13).

THE CALLING OF THE DISCIPLES
AND MIGHTY WORKS IN WORD AND DEED
(1:14—3:12)

That the calling of the two pairs of brothers at the Sea of Galilee is recounted immediately after the proclamation of the good news (1 : 14f.) is not by chance, nor does it occur out of historical considerations. It can hardly be the first meeting of Jesus with these fishermen who are to become " fishers of men " (cf. in contrast Jn. 1 : 35–51). It is, rather, an exemplary and at the same time a theologically significant calling of the disciples. The call to follow him is linked to the demand " be converted " and " believe in the gospel " (1 : 15) by an internal necessity, and the band of disciples is meant to be present from the beginning of Jesus' ministry of salvation. His community belongs to the Messiah. The first disciples must in the future build the church and in the earthly ministry of Jesus they represent the church as they listen to his words and are companions of his deeds. Thus a first section emerges extending to the second disciple-pericope, the selection of the twelve (3 : 13–19). It comprises the mighty beginning of the public life of Jesus (1 : 14–19) and a chapter concerning the authority of the God-sent bringer of salvation (2 : 1—3 : 12).

The Beginnings of the Saving Ministry
of Jesus (1:14–45)

The first chapter, which we end with Mark 1 : 45 because a new and special composition begins there (the "conflict stories"), contains the proclamation of the good news of salvation (1 : 14f.) and the "calling of the disciples" (1 : 16–20), which together make a basic introductory section. After that there is an account of Jesus in Capernaum, which on the surface puts on record "a day in the life of Jesus" but, in fact, it contains a deeper aim, namely, to throw light on Jesus' authority in teaching, his victory over the demons, his healing of the sick, and to feature preaching as his greatest concern, a "Capernaum composition" (1 : 21–39) probably put together at an early stage. Finally, there is the healing of a leper, which is significant for the "Messiah secret of Jesus" in Mark's gospel, the attempt to keep his Messiahship a secret (1 : 40–45). In this chapter Mark's portrayal of Christ already emerges in all clarity for the reader and the characteristic features of the behavior and actions of Jesus are concisely etched before his eyes.

Jesus' Message of Salvation (1 :14–15)

[14]And after John was arrested, Jesus came into Galilee, preaching the gospel of God, [15]and saying, " The time is fulfilled, and the kingdom of God is at hand; be converted and believe in the gospel."

Jesus appears as a "preacher"; the "gospel of God" cannot be brought home to man in any other way. It is not a doctrine (even though Jesus "taught" the people much in the synagogues and in the open) as, for instance, the interpretation of scriptures by the Jewish doctors of the law or the lecture of a philosopher which appeals to the intellect and insight of the audience. It is, rather, a message with a clear content which God himself commissions through a spokesman at a definite time: "the time is fulfilled and the kingdom of God is at hand." Every word is important here. The time of fulfillment looks back to a time of expectation. It is the time of salvation promised by the Old Testament spokesmen of God, the prophets, that has now arrived.

This is the *beginning* of the final ("eschatological") time, a time of God's love and light. That the "end," the "consummation," has not come yet can be inferred from the words: the kingdom of God *is at hand*. To construe this to mean that the kingdom of God is in fact already there is hardly possible in view of the Greek expression. It means "to come near," admittedly with the tense form "to have come near," so that this "nearness" is a firm and, at the same time, tangible fact. How this is meant can only be understood if one also reflects on the matter of which it is predicated: the "kingdom of God." This is a concept with a long, meaningful history. Essential for its understanding is that God *reigns* as king. The "kingdom of God" or the "royal sovereignty," the "kingship" of God, as it can also be translated, is, therefore, no institution, nor definable space, nor fixed area; on the contrary, it is more like an event, the realization of a divine act. God has always "reigned" in various ways: in creation, in history, and especially in the guidance of the people of his covenant. But here something special is meant: the perfect reign of God as the prophets had proclaimed and promised for the "end of the ages." This consummated kingdom of God which is to be announced as a divine reign of blessing over Israel and all peoples is what Jesus has in mind when he speaks, without further explanation, of the kingdom of God.

Is Jesus announcing the end of the prevailing world? If God

intends to bring about unlimited sovereignty, should not the old world with its suffering and darkness, its sin and human need, come to an end? That is an important question for the understanding of Jesus' message. He actually did proclaim that the kingdom of God is " at hand," but not calculable in terms of time. He says nothing about an immediate transformation of the prevailing world conditions. Yet he knows that something new is dawning, that from now on God will grant humanity healing and salvation in a novel and singular way. Jesus' entire ministry is meant to illustrate this new action of God: his healing of the sick and casting out of demons, his forgiving of sins and compassion for all men. Thus in the work of Jesus there already exists a *presence of the kingdom of God,* a presence of salvation: this is the " secret of the kingdom of God " (4:11). The future reality approaches men and asks them if they understand the signs. In the conversion of men, in the following of the disciples, in the gathering of the community of salvation, God's reign is also effective. The " nearness " of God becomes tangible. Hence his kingdom has come, although its presence is not yet cosmic.

This *gospel of God,* which excludes no one, not even notorious lawbreakers, publicans, and prostitutes, and which is especially proclaimed to the poor and heavily burdened, is a warm light in the cold world of hate, envy, wickedness, and violence, a ray of hope which Jesus sends into depressed and despairing hearts. But when God gives, he expects a response. His mercy is not weakness, but a call to a like response. His love demands a like love: for himself and for one's fellow men (12:30f.). That is why the joyful news of God's will to save is followed by the demand for conversion and faith in the gospel.

Conversion is much more than a " change of heart," although this is presupposed. " Penance " is also too little if one thinks it to mean a reparation of injustice or an exercise of renunciation and atonement, although such externals may also have a part to play. The Old Testament idea of " conversion " means to make an aboutface on the wrong road, that is to say: to return to God, having turned away from him. Moral failings, wickedness towards his fellows, injustice, and vice drive man away from God; he is then fleeing from God. He seeks only himself, wants to become his own master, and put himself in God's place. " How can you say, ' we are wise, . . .' The wise men are put to shame, they shall be dismayed and taken; lo, they have rejected the word of the Lord and what wisdom is in them? " says Jeremiah, the greatest prophet of conversion in the old covenant (Jer. 8:8f.). " Conversion " is what the prophets right up to John have again and again called for and have clarified in the respective situations. Often it was a turning from the worship of idols and moral collapse which was needed. Then they demanded penance and atonement for the infidelity to God. Above all, however, they were anxious about a change of heart, an inner turning to God in purity, humility, and confidence. He who was converted must learn once more to regard himself as God's creature and allow God to dispose of him.

With Jesus the call to conversion obtains its special character in the message of salvation which he proclaims at the eschatological hour. It is combined with the demand to *believe* in the gospel. Those who want to " be converted " in Jesus' sense must first of all say a heartfelt and joyful Yes to God's offer of salvation, and accept with faith the message of Jesus. There is a vigorous conversion in faith; everything else grows out of this conversion to faith. The lack of will to " be converted " for which Jesus reproaches the Galilean cities (Mt. 11:21ff.) is a lack of faith. Mark does not record any such prophetic warnings and

threats by Jesus, but Jesus' disciples preach " conversion " (6:12).
The programmatic words at the beginning state that conversion
is necessary for belief and that conversion is realized through
belief in the gospel of God. The two are bound up together.

The Calling of the Disciples (1:16–20)

*16And passing along the Sea of Galilee, he saw Simon and
Andrew the brother of Simon casting a net in the sea; for they
were fishermen. 17And Jesus said to them, " Follow me and I will
make you become fishers of men." 18And immediately they left
their nets and followed him. 19And going a little farther he saw
James the son of Zebedee and John his brother, who were in
their boats mending the nets. 20And immediately he called them;
and they left their father Zebedee in the boat with the hired
servants, and followed him.*

Matters won't rest with the general proclamation of Jesus' message of salvation; Jesus proceeds to act and calls disciples. Conversion and faith are to be realized in the *following of Jesus*; this
is the full response to the call of Jesus. The calling of the first
four disciples at the Sea of Galilee has as its purpose not only to
capture a scene from the early ministry of Jesus but has a typical
character and theological significance. Viewed historically, it was
not the first encounter of Jesus with these two pairs of brothers
whose earthly calling was to be fishermen. We know from the
gospel according to John that Jesus had already met them as
pupils of John and that the first contact took place at the place
of baptism in Judea (cf. Jn. 1:35–51). What Mark portrays is the
definite calling to discipleship in the fullest sense, and the portrayal reveals all the features of the decisive act of setting out to
follow Jesus.

The action comes from Jesus. Three factors clarify the event. Jesus looks at these men and immediately he *calls* them to himself (v. 20ᵃ). The call of God's envoy is the call of God himself; it is categorical, powerful, penetrating. When God calls, there is no hesitation. The contents of the call is the command to *follow Jesus*. To begin with, that is meant literally: the master in his ways and wanderings goes ahead of the disciples; they " follow " him, allow him to lead them. This " following " (v. 18), which in an external sense is often said of the throngs of people, has in the case of the " disciple " another, deeper spiritual meaning: he enters into a common life with the master, who from now on determines his life and ambitions, gives him doctrine and direction, also traces out his earthly path for him and gives him a share in his tasks.

The aim of the disciple's calling is expressed in symbolic words aptly chosen for these fishermen: I will make you become *fishers of men* (v. 17). This reference to the present livelihood of the disciples is neither accidental nor studied; it is, rather, a metaphor which testifies to Jesus' impressive power of language. Called by Jesus to follow him, these men are to exchange their present earthly jobs for a higher one: from now on they are to " catch " men with Jesus, to win them over to God and his kingdom. This discloses the original meaning of discipleship: a closer union with Jesus in order to share his life and to help him with his preaching (cf. 6:7–13). The disciple of Jesus must be ready to take upon himself all the consequences of this following, even to carry the cross with Jesus and to lose his life for Jesus' sake (8:34f.). When in the young church an earthly life-fellowship, vocation, and fate with Jesus were no longer possible, the spiritual meaning of the " following of Christ " alone was retained and the condition of discipleship was extended to all the faithful. All confessors of Christ were to " follow " their Master who was now exalted in heaven. His words on earth retained their binding power and one was still assured a fellowship with him without his physical, earthly presence. That is how the young church read Jesus' words and admonitions in a new light, that is to say, they referred them to themselves and to every individual.

The reaction of the first-called disciples acquires a permanent and actual significance. Again three factors are important: *immediately* Simon and Andrew leave their nets (v. 18), and afterwards James and John, the sons of Zebedee, also leave their father and the hired servants in order to join Jesus. The call of Jesus and God demands immediate and absolute obedience (cf. also Lk. 9:59–62). The pairs of brothers *leave* their present work, the sons of Zebedee their father and their family. Luke says in his account, adapted from another source ("a great catch of fish"): "They left everything and followed him " (Lk. 5:11). The call to follow Jesus basically demands a " leave-taking " from and renunciation of earthly goods for the sake of God's kingdom, even though the call affects the individual differently depending on his life-circumstances and his duties. The negative aspect of the " leave-taking " is lost in the positive: they are allowed to walk behind Jesus, to *follow* him. It is a distinction to be received into a close fellowship with God's envoy and anointed One. In spite of hostility and death, his way promises all his followers a fullness of life, for all renunciations and privations, a hundredfold reward (8:35f.; 10:17, 23ff., 29f.). The disciples, in a narrower sense, the proclaimers of the gospel, share not only the poor life of their Master but also his powers and joys (cf. 6:7–13).

On the Sabbath in the Synagogue at Capernaum (1 :21–28)

²¹*And they went to Capernaum; and immediately on the sabbath he entered the synagogue and taught.* ²²*And they were astonished at his teaching, for he taught them as one who had authority, and not as the scribes.* ²³*And immediately there was in their synagogue a man with an unclean spirit;* ²⁴*and he cried out, " What have you to do with us, Jesus of Nazareth? Have you come to destroy us? I know who you are, the Holy One of God."* ²⁵*But Jesus rebuked him saying, " Be silent and come out of him! "* ²⁶*And the unclean spirit, convulsing him and crying with a loud voice, came out of him.* ²⁷*And they were all amazed, so that they questioned among themselves, saying, " What is this? A new teaching! With authority he commands even the unclean spirits, and they obey him."* ²⁸*And at once his fame spread everywhere throughout all the surrounding region of Galilee.*

Jesus enters Capernaum with the disciples " and immediately " on the sabbath he taught in the synagogue. Without delay and with singleness of purpose Jesus goes to work, as Mark indicates with his characteristic " and immediately " (1 : 21, 23, 28, 29 and other places). The evangelist often speaks of the *teaching of Jesus,* and the disciples also adopt this work (6 : 30, only in Mark) —an indication that the Christian community knows that it is involved too. Of the content of the " teaching," for which Matthew and Luke give the great example of the " sermon on the mount," we hear nothing yet. Mark unfolds the teaching of Jesus later in the parables (4 : 1f.); but there too he is more concerned with its impact as a dividing force among the audience. What Jesus " taught " the Jewish audience on earth at that time, probably interpretations of the law, a new understanding of

God's will, is recorded insofar as it affects Christian life; but that too can be imparted later (cf. 7:17–23; 10:1–45; 12:13–37).

To begin with, it is enough that we know of the earthly appearance of Jesus, that he *taught with divine authority* and not like the scribes. The latter held to their teaching tradition, the "tradition of the elders" (7:3), and often, according to Jesus' judgment, they failed to do God's original will for the sake of human interpretations and precepts (cf. 7:6–13). Jesus teaches with absolute authority and gives his own interpretation of the text (10:5–9), and in this he proves himself to be plenipotentiary of God, just as he does in the casting out of demons. The two things Jesus does in the synagogue of Capernaum, teaching with authority and casting out impure spirits, mean but one thing for Mark, namely, evidence of Jesus' power, which makes men "astonished" (v. 22) and amazed (v. 27). They sense the newness of what is happening. The teaching word, full of authority, and the word of exorcism, full of power, are both equally a sign that God's kingdom is at hand.

Thus the casting out of an unclean spirit which "immediately" followed, told in accordance with the mentality of the time, must also be understood as evidence of the *power* bestowed on Jesus. A poor tortured man is freed from a terrible suffering which is attributed to an "unclean spirit." In some texts (1:32; 3:10f.; 6:13) a distinction is made between the sick and the possessed; at the very least the latter betray especially serious pathological symptoms. For the evangelist the ungodly power of the evil one, of Satan, stands behind the unclean spirits (cf. 3:22ff.). The adversary of God and of Jesus (1:13) summons all his might to put a stop to Jesus' ministry of salvation and the inception of God's kingdom. But Jesus proves to be the stronger (3:27) and repulses Satan's kingdom. The first detailed description of an exorcism already assures victory to God and the superiority of Jesus.

The dialogue between Jesus and the impure spirit (who also speaks for others like himself) clarifies the combat between the two opponents. The demon senses the presence of the Mighty One who wants to rob him of his " dwelling," to tear the human victim away from him, and cries out words of adjuration. The loud cry and the defiant questions are aimed at warding off the attack of the exorcist: " What have you to do with us? . . . Have you come to destroy us?" Articulating the name (" Jesus of Nazareth "), declaring " I know who you are," the numinous title " the Holy One of God " are not respectful confessions or furtive pleas; on the contrary, they are " name magic," attempts to gain control over the exorcist through the disclosure of his name and title. In ancient (also Jewish) history of exorcism the exorcist makes a counterattack and tries with adjuration formulas and magic means to master the demon, to force him to leave the possessed man. Against the background of such an approach the originality and uniqueness of Jesus' actions in the spectators' eyes of that time become apparent. Jesus does without magic words and magic means and commands the unclean spirit with a mere word of command: " Be silent and come out of him!" He simply commands and the spirits must obey (cf. v. 27). Such *effective words* are a sign that God is at work.

Further Activity in Capernaum and Departure (1 :29–39)

²⁹*And immediately he left the synagogue and entered the house of Simon and Andrew, with James and John.* ³⁰*Now Simon's mother-in-law lay sick with a fever, and immediately they told*

him of her. [31]*And he came and took her by the hand and lifted her up, and the fever left her; and she served them.*

After the first sensational performance in the synagogue Jesus goes to the house of Simon and Andrew. It seems that he wants to be alone there. But his disciples immediately come with a concern: Simon's mother-in-law is suffering from a fever, and he does not hesitate to cure her. In the case of dangerous illnesses the sabbatical laws, also according to the Rabbis, need not be observed. He takes the sick woman by the hand and lifts her up. The woman rises and gives the men hospitality, a sign that the fever has truly left her. This brief narrative still shows the freshness of original experience. It is Mark's *first* account of the *healing of the sick* and spans a bridge to the others which Jesus undertakes after sundown, that is, after the sabbath.

This ancient account aims at presenting Jesus as healer of the sick. This activity also belongs to his ministry but is not his main concern, as the conclusion shows. One can discern a graded evaluation: more important than the healing of all kinds of infirmities is the casting out of demons (v. 34[b]) since they show more clearly that Satan's power is being broken and God's kingdom is coming. The most important matter, however, is the preaching of Jesus, since by means of it the aim of his mission (v. 38) is made public and the call of God reaches mankind directly. For Jesus the healings of the sick stand in the same light: they too are *signs of the salvation* which God offers mankind. But they bring with them the danger that mankind will remain attached to externals and strive only to remove its earthly needs, will not reflect on the deeper meaning of the event and interpret God's salvific aims falsely. For Jesus it is something like a temptation to let himself be carried away on the waves of the people's enthusiasm. He seeks solitude as he did after his baptism, where he prayerfully reflects on his real mission, and he abruptly breaks short his stay in Capernaum.

[32]That evening, at sundown, they brought to him all who were sick or possessed with demons. [33]And the whole city was gathered together about the door. [34]And he healed many who were sick with various diseases, and cast out many demons; and he would not permit the demons to speak, because they knew him.

The healings in the evening, when the sabbath was over, are described graphically in verse 33. Knowing that Jesus was in Simon's house, the people waited until the end of the sabbath so as not to break the sabbatical regulations by carrying biers. Now they bring along all their sick and possessed and the entire city congregates before the door of the house. Jesus healed *many who were sick*. This is not meant in any restrictive sense, as if to define a limit to his power. The " many " healings illustrate the magnitude of his help; they do not signify that all earthly sufferings are to be banished. The healings are intended to be signs of God's compassion, but the people do not understand this and seek only further help (v. 37). Augmenting, the evangelist mentions many more castings out of demons, but adds that Jesus does not permit the demons to speak, " because they knew him." He does not want the testimony of the demons precisely because theirs are demonic voices (cf. v. 24). It is preferable that people should come to think for themselves by witnessing God's saving deeds and thus come to understand the meaning of Jesus' actions. All external happenings stand in a twilight; believing reflection is necessary to order them into the meaningful context of divine thought. Faith masters the ambiguity of history.

[35]*And in the morning, a great while before day, he rose and went out to a lonely place, and there he prayed.* [36]*And Simon and those who were with him followed him,* [37]*and they found him and said to him, " Everyone is searching for you." * [38]*And he said to them, " Let us go on to the next towns, that I may preach there also; for that is why I came out." * [39]*And he went throughout all Galilee preaching in their synagogues and casting out demons.*

Faced with external success, the influx of people, Jesus himself wants to think clearly about the commission of his Father and goes into solitude to pray. The early hour, for it is still dark, indicates, perhaps, an inner struggle, similar to the temptation of Satan, from which Jesus as man is not free. But his union with God, quickened and strengthened *in prayer*, leads him to find the right way with inner assurance. When his disciples, thinking in human terms like the others or, more correctly, not thinking at all, lacking the inner alertness of their master, come to bring him back, he is firm in his decision: " Let us go to the next towns, that I may preach there also; for that is why I came out." It is one of those pronouncements which disclose Jesus' awareness of his mission. The young church grasped it in sharper contours clarified by her belief in Christ: Jesus' urge to preach, his will to bring God's message of salvation to all his people without placing himself at the center, confirmed by his behavior, his wanderings about Galilee, is an unmistakable testimony to his spirit. The young church could well have given greater prominence to his extraordinary deeds and his self-*consciousness*, but she testifies to Jesus' selfless service to preaching, his fidelity to the task God imparted to him. Certainly Jesus becomes for her a great example for her preachers who have taken on the same task as their Master.

The concluding verse is a short summary of the beginning of Jesus' ministry. It shows again and more emphatically the viewpoint and interpretation of the evangelist. In preaching and casting out demons Jesus prepares the way for the approaching kingdom of God. As in Capernaum he initially keeps to the synagogues, and what Mark wishes to say is that Jesus behaves as he did on that sabbath of which he has just told us (1:21–27). Not only is the fame of Jesus now spread throughout the surrounding region (v. 28) but the *fame of God* himself penetrates through Jesus into all the localities of Galilee. The gospel is beginning its triumphal course.

The Healing of a Leper (1:40–45)

⁴⁰*And a leper came to him beseeching him, and kneeling said to him, "If you will, you can make me clean." ⁴¹Moved with pity, he stretched out his hand and touched him, and said to him, "I will; be clean." ⁴²And immediately the leprosy left him, and he was made clean. ⁴³And he sternly charged him, and sent him away at once, ⁴⁴and said to him, "See that you say nothing to anyone; but go show yourself to the priest, and offer for your cleansing what Moses commanded, for a proof to the people." ⁴⁵But he went out and began to talk freely about it, and to spread the news, so that Jesus could no longer openly enter a town, but was out in the country; and people came to him from every quarter.*

Much thought has been given to, and much has been written about the so-called "Messiah secret" in Mark's gospel, that is to say, the desire of Jesus to keep his " Messiahship " a secret. The designation is not happy, for in the whole of the first part of Mark's gospel the question concerning the " Messiah," in the sense of the current expectation of a theocratic messiah king, the " son of David," does not enter in at all. The people do not seem to think on these lines. It is more likely that Mark is pursuing a Christological line for his Christian readers : Jesus wants to conceal his own *majesty and divinity* and fulfill his preaching commission only as the obedient servant of God, and yet a powerful force goes out from him and people throng to him frantically. The evangelist, who with his readers believes in the glory of the exalted Lord and understands that his Sonship of God is the true reason for the astounding earthly ministry of Jesus, wants to make clear that before his resurrection Jesus conceals his glory intentionally because he wants to go the path of humility, taking on suffering and the cross. On earth Jesus is anxious to avoid any notice that his person would arouse so as to be only the herald of the gospel.

This explains several apparent contradictions : Jesus goes to all the towns of Galilee in order to preach (1 : 39) and flees from the thronging of the crowd to a place of solitude (1 : 45). He heals the leper and commands him to show himself to a priest " for a proof to the people " (v. 44) and yet he charges him sternly not to say anything about it to anyone. Later he withdraws to the sea with his disciples (3 : 7), but when the people once more throng about him he again heals many but forbids the demons to let him be known (3 : 10ff.). He wants to gather the people to himself, and he elects the twelve and sends them out in pairs (6 : 7–13); then he withdraws with the disciples (6 : 30f.), but once again he has compassion on the throng who follow him into the wilderness (6 : 34ff.).

Jesus appeared as contradictory to his contemporaries: a powerful proclaimer of God, a miracle-worker and healer to whom people came in crowds, and yet a man who kept a peculiar distance from the people and remained incomprehensible to mankind. But the evangelist makes it clear to his readers, who believe in the crucified and risen Christ, that the earthly Jesus had to behave in this way. The powers dwelling within him had their source in the *mystery of his divine Sonship* which, however, was not revealed till his resurrection. On earth he had to tread the path of the obedient servant of God which acquires its meaning only in the light of the resurrection. Thus the " secret of the Messiahship," better, the secret of his divine Sonship, represents only the solution of believers to the riddle which Jesus' behavior and conduct posed to his contemporaries.

If one reads the remarkable, apparently contradictory *healing of a leper* from this vantage point, then much that would be obscure is made more apparent. To begin with, we have a scene which is fully understandable as the history of a healing: a poor, ostracized man afflicted with leprosy dares to approach Jesus, and falling on his knees beseeches him with great confidence: " If you will, you can make me clean." And Jesus has pity on his need. If one prefers the variant, " he was angry," because it is harsh and inexplicable, the " anger " of Jesus would not refer to the man who acts against the law but to the power of evil which had delivered him up to death. For without any discernible change of mood Jesus stretches out his hand (a gesture of healing) and even touches the " untouchable " and grants his request with corresponding words: " I will; be clean." At this mere word of authority the healing takes place without delay.

Only the subsequent behavior of Jesus presents a riddle: sternly threatening, Jesus drives the cured man away, sends him to the priest that he be declared clean and present the prescribed offering for the cleansing. " For a proof to the people " is added, perhaps not only that the man give a proof of his cure before the people, but also that it become, in the gospel sense, a *testimony to God* for non-believers (cf. 6:11; 13:9). Then, here too the evangelist would have broken through the " historical " plane of thinking.

The whole story seems to have been written largely for later readers, as verse 45 once more confirms. The healed man who spreads the news receives no blame. After Easter Jesus' deed can be understood properly: Jesus gives health and life to a man dedicated to death. But in those days Jesus concealed himself from the people, although they streamed to him from all sides. He was a light that could not remain hidden, although the people did not understand this light. All this had to be so, because Jesus was obliged to walk obediently the path through darkness to glory.

The Full Authority of God's Envoy (2:1—3:6)

The next five pericopes present in their manner a new unity which Mark probably found already in existence. From a systematic-historical point of view they are usually labeled as the " Galilean conflict stories " because they contain the stories of Jesus' conflict with opponents. Their aim is not so much to portray episodes from Jesus' ministry as to set forth answers to definite questions. That is why they culminate in each case in a declaration from Jesus which is full of meaning (2:10, 17, 19, 28; 3:4). Although correctly observed, one must inquire further why the evangelist has inserted these stories in this place. Again he is concerned with the portrait and the significance of Jesus for the Christian community. Jesus' majesty shines forth, he acts and decides in a manner which is new and exciting, which provokes contradiction, and he finally incurs for himself the deadly hatred of the leading class (3 : 6).

But the intention of the evangelist goes beyond this: in those fundamental sentences which mark the climax of the pericopes, Jesus also speaks of the meaning of his mission and of the saving authority bestowed on him. The lasting significance of these words which articulate something about the person and the saving ministry of Jesus is to be assimilated by the Christian community for its faith and its life.

The Full Authority of the Son of Man to Forgive Sins on Earth (2:1-12)

¹*And when he returned to Capernaum after some days, it was reported that he was at home.* ²*And many were gathered together, so that there was no longer room for them, not even about the door; and he was preaching the word to them.* ³*And they came, bringing to him a paralytic carried by four men.* ⁴*And when they could not get near him because of the crowd, they removed the roof above him; and when they had made an opening they let down the pallet on which the paralytic lay.* ⁵*And when Jesus saw their faith, he said to the paralytic, " My son, your sins are forgiven."* ⁶*Now some of the scribes were sitting there, questioning in their hearts,* ⁷*" Why does this man speak thus? It is blasphemy! Who can forgive sins but God alone? "* ⁸*And immediately Jesus perceived in his spirit that they thus ques-*

tioned within themselves, and said to them, " Why do you question thus in your hearts? [9]Which is easier to say to the paralytic, ' Your sins are forgiven,' or to say, ' Rise, take up your pallet and walk '? [10]But that you may know that the Son of man has authority on earth to forgive sins "—he said to the paralytic —[11]" I say to you, rise, take up your pallet and go home." [12]And he rose, and immediately took up his pallet and went out before them all; so that they were all amazed and glorified God, saying, " We never saw anything like this! "

On the surface we are dealing here with a description of the healing of a sick man which because of its circumstances has become unforgettable. Jesus, once again " at home " in Capernaum, is " besieged " by a great throng; but the men who bring a paralytic on a pallet to have him healed by Jesus know what to do. They remove the rafters and dig up the clay roof of the simple house, and through the opening they let down the helpless invalid in front of Jesus. In the end Jesus speaks the saving words: " I say to you, rise, take up your pallet and go home " (v. 11). But another event is inserted into this account. In the center we have *Jesus forgiving sins,* which arouses abusive thoughts in the scribes, who observe him with suspicion. Jesus proves the authority of the " Son of man " to forgive sins on earth (v. 10) and that is for the young church what is of lasting significance in this story.

The healing of the sick and the forgiving of sins are related; to the Jewish way of thinking there is even a causal connection : they regarded serious illness as a *consequence of sin.* When Jesus, to begin with, speaks the word of forgiveness, the deeper root of the evil is removed. The liberation from corporeal infirmity means the consummation of the " healing " and, at the same time, the proof that the man's sins are forgiven. Further, the proof of Jesus' authority to forgive sins proceeds according to the Jewish way of thinking, that is, as a conclusion from the "greater to the smaller." If Jesus accomplishes the—humanly speaking—"more difficult," namely, the bodily healing which can be observed and checked, he demonstrates thereby that the "easier," the absolution of the man's sins, was no empty word. Thus Jesus confronts his critics on their own ground and defeats them with their own weapons; for would God have given a "blasphemer" the power of restoring the health of a seriously lamed man?

The question in verse 9, however, gives one food for thought: is it truly *easier,* is it a lesser matter to declare a man free of his sin than to free him from his bodily infirmities? The community knows that the former deed of Jesus is mightier—and it continues to occur in their midst through the word of forgiveness by the full authority of the risen Christ (cf. Jn. 20:22f.). For the community, Jesus' healing on earth becomes only a sign of the full salvation which God promises and of which it already partakes. Not only at the end, at the consummation, will God's salvation become reality. It already begins now on earth, although stripped of outward show in the miracles of forgiveness. God turns mercifully towards sinful mankind, who is in need of salvation, reconciles him with himself, and thereby inaugurates the whole saving process for mankind and the world.

This also severs the causal connection between sin and illness. For not all those whose sins are forgiven arrive at bodily health; this is something over and above which Jesus does in the case of the lame man. But not every illness in the gospel is attributed to sin. In the case of the man born blind to whom Jesus restores his eyesight he expressly rejects this idea (Jn. 9:3). In this the

Christian community has departed from Jewish ideas. For the community, true salvation lies in *reconciliation with God,* which occurs in the absolution from sin, and that is the lasting doctrine which the community learns from this deed of Jesus.

But something else is noteworthy in the kernel sentence of this pericope: the *Son of man* has authority on earth to forgive sin. Consequently, Jesus' words to the paralytic, " My son, your sins are forgiven " (v. 5), are interpreted to mean that he himself forgives sin in God's name and does not merely express his assurance or certainty that God forgives sin. Even the scribes understand the words as a usurpation of God's sole right and, consequently, as blasphemy (2:7). Jesus' self-characterization as " Son of man " is striking. The oldest use of this mysterious title certainly lies in the eschatological (referring to the end of the world) utterances, that the " Son of man " will come in the clouds of heaven (13:26; 14:62; cf. Dan. 7:13f.) and exercise his function as judge (8:38). It is a title of majesty, so that all utterances which refer to the suffering of the " Son of man " (8:31; 9:9, 31; 10:33, 45; 14:21, 41) sound strange and incomprehensible to Jewish ears, as do those which refer to the present, worldly might of the " Son of man " (2:10, 28). These are exclusively Christian ideas which became possible only in view of Jesus and his special Messiahship. This meaningful title sheds more light on the assertion of verse 10: because Jesus is the " Son of man " who will come in glory, he can already exercise on earth the divine right to forgive sin. In him future power is already present, not that of a judge who punishes but of one who mercifully forgives.

That Jesus intended to bring mankind the forgiveness of God and that through it God's saving love of the world was to be made manifest is confirmed by *Jesus' attitude towards sinners* (cf. 2:13-17). What seemed offensive to the Jews in those days is affirmed by the young church in its faith in Christ: that the powers of salvation are present even in the earthly Jesus, that he pronounces his word of forgiveness with divine authority. But she also knows that his word of grace retains its efficacy in the church through the entire history of the world until the " Son of man " will be revealed in glory.

At Table with Tax Collectors and Sinners (2 :13–17)

¹³He went out again beside the sea; and all the crowd gathered about him, and he taught them. ¹⁴And as he passed on he saw Levi the son of Alphaeus sitting at the tax office, and he said to him, " Follow me." And he rose and followed him. ¹⁵And as he sat at table in his house, many tax collectors and sinners were sitting with Jesus and his disciples; for there were many who followed him. ¹⁶And the scribes of the Pharisees, when they saw that he was eating with sinners and tax collectors, said to his disciples, " Why does he eat with tax collectors and sinners?" ¹⁷And when Jesus heard it he said to them, " Those who are well have no need of a physician, but those who are sick; I came not to call the righteous, but sinners."

This pericope belongs to the theme of sin and forgiveness. In Jesus' attitude towards " sinners " and in his concluding pronouncement, the central, joyful message of the gospel stands out still more clearly: Jesus was sent especially to sinners; God wishes to demonstrate his incomprehensible mercy in them. What Jesus proclaims he also does, without fear of the criticism of men. His message becomes credible through his person, moreover: his personal behavior is the revelation of the divine will to save mankind.

The calling of another disciple is presented as an introduction. On this occasion the one called is a notorius " sinner," *the tax collector Levi* (who is also called Matthew; cf. Mt. 9:9). In accordance with the system of the day, tax collectors gathered the import and export taxes under the direction of a chief tax collector (cf. Zacchaeus in Lk. 19:10), who had to pay the ruler of the land a considerable amount in rent. Tax collectors were regarded as " sinners " even by virtue of their profession, since they had also to deal with non-Jews and " defiled " themselves in doing so. In addition they had the ill-repute of enriching themselves, for the most part unjustly (cf. Lk. 19:8). Together with some other professions, they were ostracized as lawbreakers and hated by the people on account of their occupation. Jesus sets himself above such considerations. As he did to the fishermen beside the sea, Jesus calls Levi-Matthew away from his present livelihood to follow him as a disciple, and the despised tax collector follows after him. The evangelist does not make much ado about this; the disciple is known to his readers. The fact, however, that he does not close his mind to the call of Jesus justifies the " divine risk " in squandering confidence, in calling sinners.

Then there is a banquet, in whose house is not certain. Luke mentions Levi as the host, and so it would have been historically. For Jesus often accepted invitations, and this earned for him the spiteful reproach of a " glutton and a drunkard " (Mt. 11:19 = Lk. 7:34). In Mark the " in his house " could also refer to the house in which Jesus lived (cf. 1:29; 2:1), in which case Jesus would have invited the tax collectors—still more scandalous for the guardian of morals. Jesus as host: what a significant aspect for the listening community! But we need not accept such an interpretation. Simple narrative art is often inexact in details, and the calling of Levi is but an introduction to the new scene.

Jesus is at table with " sinners and tax collectors," which is against the law for the scribes of the Pharisees (a special group within the " brotherhood ") because Jesus is making himself one with " sinners " and so " defiles " himself. The Pharisees immediately reproach his disciples with this. Jesus, who hears of it, answers in a proverbial type of saying which disarms his critics more successfully than long speeches: *those who are well have no need of a physician, but those who are sick*. Such words of popular and profane wisdom uttered by him are transmitted to us also in other places. Why should he not have used them to clarify God's thoughts? A " missionary phrase " (" I came . . .") is added which expresses clearly the matter of Jesus' concern. Jesus is aware of being sent to call sinners and not the righteous.

That Jesus turns to sinners remains a deep *mystery*. According to the portrait that Mark sketches he is a man bound with the closest bonds to God, but God knows of human sin and guilt, of the need and poverty of human existence. Precisely because of his union with God, of his inner knowledge of God's thoughts and aims, Jesus approaches sinners and " eats with them," which for the oriental calls forth a picture of friendly, harmonious companionship.

This meal is also a witness to the *humanity* of Jesus. He comes close to mankind in communal eating and drinking, he speaks with all and does not seek exclusive company. For him there is no division between " saints " and " sinners." He knows that people who have experienced the incompleteness of " worldly " life are not seldom ready for the call of God. Sinners who have tasted the wretchedness of sin are often capable of a greater love of God and man than petty observers of the law. For all that, Jesus' divine-human love of sinners remains a mystery. According to the wording, he does not condemn the righteous; but they do not " need " him as do the sick, the ostracized, the sinners. Something of the irrational *love* of the Old Testament God is in evidence here, who in spite of all the faithlessness of the people of the covenant does not desert them, but draws them to himself again and again with incomprehensible compassion.

There is a hidden dialectic in Jesus' words, he is aware of being sent to *all* mankind and he demands conversion of *all* (1 : 15). All those who wish to share in his saving love and divine compassion must regard themselves as sinners before God. Thus the " tax collectors and sinners " represent all of mankind who open their minds in faith to the message of salvation.

"Fasting" and the Time of Salvation (2 :18–22)

[18]*Now John's disciples and the Pharisees were fasting; and people came and said to him, " Why do John's disciples and the disciples of the Pharisees fast, but your disciples do not fast? "* [19]*And Jesus said to them, " Can the wedding guests fast while the bridegroom is with them? As long as they have the bridegroom with them, they cannot fast.* [20]*The days will come when the bridegroom is taken away from them, and then they will fast in that day.* [21]*No one sews a piece of unshrunk cloth on an old garment; if he does the patch tears away from it, the new from the old, and a new tear is made.* [22]*And no one puts new wine into old wineskins; if he does, the wine will burst the skins,*

and the wine is lost, and so are the skins; but new wine is for fresh skins."

For orientals a wedding meant a time of great jubilation. Many guests came, especially the invited friends of the bridegroom, the " sons of the bridal chamber," who were expected to contribute to the joy and merriment of the bridal couple. The wedding becomes a *metaphor for the time of salvation,* as it is written in the book of Isaiah: " As the bridegroom rejoices over the bride, so shall your God rejoice over you " (Is. 62:5; cf. 61:10). In rabbinical theology this metaphor is retained, even heightened, by the allegorical construction of the relation between Yahweh and Israel in the Song of Solomon. Thus Jesus indicates that his presence heralds the time of salvation in which God's joyful promise is being fulfilled. In this time it is inconceivable that the wedding guests should " fast," or " mourn," as Matthew puts it (9:15). The joy of salvation which the presence and nearness of Jesus diffuses must also find an echo in the behavior of his disciples. Wedding jubilation does not go with fasting and mourning for the dead. The young church has understood this doctrine and has intoned the eschatological jubilation in her divine service; her eucharistic celebrations, in the framework of a communal meal, bore a joyful stamp: " They partook of bread with glad and generous hearts " (Acts 2:46).

And yet there is another aspect which leads to *mourning and lamentation of the dead.* The words linked to the metaphor of the wedding (v. 20) speak of days when " the bridegroom is taken away from the wedding guests." For the young church Jesus himself was the bridegroom and she also recalled his *death.* But that is only, as it were, an incidental remark, since the subsequent parables deal only with the new which the present time brings. Jesus' coming signifies a radical change, and the basic mood of the new time is God-given joy. This truth lived on in the young church, although it came under a certain check and restriction because of Jesus' death: now, in the meantime, until Jesus' final coming in glory one must also commemorate the death of the Lord. His " absence " is a separation from him and a reason for mourning as it painfully reminds one that one is tied to this world. Worldly existence also demands a separation from seductive joys and an endurance of deprivations and sufferings if one hopes to achieve full joy with the Lord. This tension explains the divergent attitudes of the later church towards penance (up to the more recent high regard for the observance of fasting) and the joy of salvation.

The last two verses are a double parable which illustrates the same thought: with Jesus something entirely *new*, which is no longer compatible with the old, has entered the world. Where the prophets speak of the " new," it refers to the new creation of God and the new order of the final time. According to Jeremiah, God wishes to make a " new covenant " with Israel by putting his law within them and writing it in their hearts (Jer. 31 : 31ff.); according to Ezekiel, giving them a new heart and putting a new spirit within them (Ezek. 36 : 26); according to Isaiah, creating a new heaven and a new earth (Is. 65 : 17; 66 : 22).

The Son of Man, Lord of the Sabbath (2 :23–28)

[23]*One sabbath he was going through the grainfields; and as they made their way his disciples began to pluck ears of grain.* [24]*And the Pharisees said to him, " Look, why are they doing what is not lawful on the sabbath?"* [25]*And he said to them, " Have you*

*never read what David did, when he was in need and was
hungry, he and those who were with him :* [26]*how he entered the
house of God, when Abiathar was high priest, and ate the bread
of the presence, which it is not lawful for anyone but the priest
to eat, and also gave it to those who were with him?"* [27]*And he
said to them, " The sabbath was made for man and not man for
the sabbath;* [28]*so the Son of man is lord even of the sabbath."*

Again an early tradition could have linked up the new story
according to external viewpoints: " fasting " and " being
hungry " are closely associated. Just as Jesus defends his disciples'
failure to fast, so he now defends their breaking of the sabbath
to still their hunger. The dispute, however, leads to a different
climax: *the Son of man is lord of the sabbath.* Of the two state-
ments about the sabbath at the end which are set apart from the
incident itself by a new start (" And he said to them "), the first
seems to fit better into the situation and sounds humanly understandable, but the more important of the two is the second,
which makes an assertion about the " Son of man " (cf. 2 : 10).
Only the latter is also handed down to us by the other synoptists;
verse 27 is a supplementary insertion (probably from Mark) and
contains an idea which even the Jewish scribes did not contest.
The two sayings give different answers to the sabbath question,
but they are compatible for the Christian community, not,
indeed, in the manner that verse 28 could be interpreted by
verse 27 (as if the " Son of man " meant no more than " human
being " originally). The question about the sabbath remained
topical also for Jewish Christians; the decisive solution was given
by Jesus' attitude, respectively, the assertion that the Son of man
is lord also of the sabbath. Perhaps conflicts about the sabbath in
the Jewish-Christian community were the reason for handing

this down; but this disputation, which presupposes Jewish attitudes, is still very relevant to heathen-Christian readers of Mark and also to later believers.

The occasion is the passing of Jesus and his disciples through the ripening grainfields, and it occurred on a *sabbath*. Whether Jesus went ahead and the disciples, as usual, " followed " is not noted. Some have expressed the opinion that Mark did not wish to convey (as Matthew and Luke do clearly) that the disciples plucked ears of corn to still their hunger, but that they, hurrying ahead, pulled out the stalks to make a way for him—a royal path for the Messiah as the community would understand it; that Jesus is here highlighting the time of salvation, the actual fulfillment of the " sabbath," the day of God. As attractive as this explanation sounds, it does not appear to have sufficient foundation. The example of David emphasizes hunger, and the custom of rubbing ripe grain and eating it is ancient in the Orient, and is tolerated if someone wants to still his hunger. Only that the disciples did this on a sabbath is a scandal to the Pharisees. The plucking of ears of grain is listed under the thirty-nine *activities forbidden* on the sabbath; it was regarded as a " work of reaping." Finally, it is not the occasion itself that is decisive but Jesus' attitude towards the alleged breaking of the sabbath.

From this story, too, an unheard of *claim of Jesus* emerges, which is clarified by Christian tradition. Here something of his " teaching with authority " (1:22) and of his free, sovereign behavior are revealed. He had often overridden sabbatical precepts which were exceedingly important to the Jews and strictly observed. In these daring and, for himself, dangerous decisions he has brought to light his exclusive union with the will of God as he recognized it with inner certainty, his freedom from the judgment of men, and his hidden majesty. Here he testifies to being " Lord of," which is also portrayed in another way in his casting out of demons and healing of the sick. The young church has understood this and recognized in it the majesty of the " Son of man." In the freedom of conscience, liberated by him yet tied to the will of God, there exists an equally joyous proclamation, as in the other statement that the Son of man has the power to forgive sin on earth (2:10). Thus it makes good sense that the two assertions about the "Son of man" in this section do not stand far apart: the forgiving of sins and the liberation from human narrow-mindedness are expressions of the same saving authority.

To Save Life (3 :1–6)

¹*Again he entered the synagogue, and a man was there who had a withered hand.* ²*And they watched him to see whether he would heal him on a sabbath, so that they might accuse him.* ³*And he said to the man who had the withered hand, " Come here."* ⁴*And he said to them, " Is it lawful on the sabbath to do good or do harm, to save life or to kill?" But they were silent.* ⁵*And he looked around at them with anger, grieved at their hardness of heart, and said to the man. " Stretch out your hand." He stretched it out and his hand was restored.* ⁶*The Pharisees went out, and immediately held counsel with the Herodians against him, how to destroy him.*

A new sabbath story, this time a healing. The theme of the previous pericope is continued, therefore, but in greater depth. Jesus' transgression of the sabbatical precept, which also for-

bade as " work " activities related to healing, is motivated by
a *concern for salvation*. His opponents are blind to this; their
minds are closed. They have hardened their hearts and oppose
the will of God in their human thinking. The last part of the
" conflict story " augments the conflict of Jesus with his opponents to such a degree that his terrible end can be surmised.
Historically speaking, the final remark (verse 6) comes too early;
but by the extreme decision to kill, the presentation aims at dis-
closing the inner situation in which Jesus finds himself vis-à-vis
his opponents. It is an irreconcilable opposition, a hardening of
the two fronts, revealed by Jesus' union with the will of God and
his opponent's " hardness " of heart in regard to God's intention to save.

The healing is told in the usual way: after the details concerning the illness—in this case a man with a " withered " hand,
bloodless and powerless—there follows Jesus' word of authority,
and after that the immediate effect is confirmed. But this account
does not take up the central position, rather, the *words of Jesus*
to his opponents watching with suspicion. Jesus asks them two
questions which are worthy of note in their sequence and
gradation. To begin with, there are the words whereby Jesus
places the duty of love above the ritual rule of law. The Pharisees
forbade any helpful endeavors for the sick undertaken on a
sabbath, except in case of a threat to life. For Jesus, however, the
duty *to do good* stands higher, and to omit the good is *to do
harm*. Then a strange sequel follows: to save life or to kill—but
this illness is in no way a threat to life!

For that reason, Jesus' *anger* and *grief* over their *hardness of
heart* is more than merely human emotion. True, it is that too,
and in it Jesus' human thoughts and feelings are revealed; but
this is founded on his union with God. What is festering in the

hearts of his opponents is a " hardness " or " stubbornness " which in biblical thought has a very serious background. According to Isaiah 6:10, God himself has hardened the hearts of the obstinate people, and Mark adopts these words of the prophet to characterize the negative effect of the parable on " those outside " (4:11f.). The saving actions and words of Jesus, which reveal him as the bringer of salvation sent by God, have the opposite effect on these men: they darken their minds with wicked thoughts even to the point of murderous intentions towards him who was sent to save them also.

A Summary of Jesus' Ministry (3:7–12)

7Jesus withdrew with his disciples to the sea, and a great multitude from Galilee followed; also from Judea 8and Jerusalem and Idumea and from beyond the Jordan and from about Tyre and Sidon a great multitude, hearing all that he did, came to him. 9And he told his disciples to have a boat ready for him because of the crowd, lest they should crush him; 10for he had healed many, so that all who had diseases pressed upon him to touch him. 11And whenever the unclean spirits beheld him, they fell down before him and cried out, " You are the Son of God." 12And he strictly ordered them not to make him known.

This concluding piece of the first section is clearly fashioned by the evangelist himself. Here he once more accentuates his main concern in the portrayal of the beginning of Jesus' ministry, and for that reason these verses are especially revealing. It is clear that he wants to show the *mighty impact* of the message and activity of Jesus in Galilee and beyond in pagan territory (vv. 7–8), just as he ends the following second section (3 : 13—6 : 6) with an entirely different scene, the rejection of Jesus in his home town, Nazareth, in order to accentuate the basic misunderstanding of the people, their concealed disbelief. But to begin with, he wishes to emphasize the tremendous thronging of people from near and far, the power of the message of salvation, the influence of Jesus' personality, the power that emanates from him, revealed in the healing of the sick and the casting out of demons, even through touch alone. For that reason he puts his summary account at the end of the first accounts, which he had constructed from tradition.

People flock to Jesus because they hear what he accomplishes; the fame of his healings and his mighty deeds draws them. It seems to be the intention of the passage to underline the passion of the crowd for miracles and its urge to obtain aid in bodily suffering. This impression, however, is deceptive; its focus is not the people but *Jesus and his behavior*. The aim is to show Jesus in his irresistible power of attraction and the power of healing emanating from him. Jesus has a boat made ready for him so as not to be too pressed upon by the people surrounding him; for they want to touch him, as later the woman who had a flow of blood, that by this alone their health might be restored (5 : 27–31). Those possessed by unclean spirits fall down before him as if his very presence forced the demons out of their victims. Their adjuring cry, whereby they disclose Jesus' secret, echoes through the crowd; but Jesus does not want to be made known by them. All this strikes us as strange, but the evangelist depicts this in line with the mentality of a time when one believed in such divine power embodied in a man and that it flowed out of him as by magic. Nevertheless, Jesus is different from those " divine men " and magical wonder-workers of his day: he does not seek sensation or ostentation, and from the reports on his miracles so far, it is clear that he heals the sick and casts out demons solely through God's mighty word.

The young church is assured of the power given to Jesus, in an illustrative fashion, in this antiquated narration. It confirms her belief that Jesus is the only *Son of God,* as the demons proclaim him to be. However, Jesus cannot and will not accept this " profession " of the unclean spirits, because it would put his Sonship in a false light. It would not be understood for what it is in the light of Easter belief. Jesus, truly God's Son (15 : 39), brings mankind to final salvation, the restoration of its existence in fellowship with God.

That which is here portrayed, with the illustrative means of an antiquated view of life, retains its significance as revelation: Jesus is the hidden source of salvation, the physician of mankind, internally ill. The power, which according to this portrayal flows externally from the earthly Jesus, is effective in a higher degree as power for salvation in the *risen* Jesus, who can and will impart to all men the power of divine life. The picture which this summary account draws of the successful ministry of Jesus by the Sea of Galilee, the earthly starting point and center of his proclamation of salvation, is, as it were, a sign of mankind gathered around the risen Jesus. To them he gives the redemptive powers of God, if they recognize him to be the physician and saviour sent to them.

THE ELECTION OF THE TWELVE, THE GATHERING OF BELIEVERS, AND THE TURNING AWAY FROM UNBELIEVERS (3:13—6:6a)

The new section, which we begin with a second important "disciple pericope," the election of the twelve, and end with Jesus' rejection in Nazareth, unfolds and deepens the themes of the previous section, advances the happenings about Jesus, and lets the uniting as well as the dividing power of the gospel be seen more clearly. A key to the understanding of what the evangelist wishes to portray here is furnished by the central piece, the parable instruction (4:1–34). The parables of Jesus about God's reign not only illuminate the contents of his message but also become a happening which separates the believers, to whom "has been given the secret of the kingdom of God," from those who "indeed see but do not perceive, indeed hear but not do understand" (4:11f.). Jesus wants to collect his community of believers and, for this purpose, he elects the "twelve," who thereby stand apart from the great multitude which (according to the summary account) thronged to him from everywhere (3:13–17). In this the reader can recognize the formation of the later community of Christ which is built on these men as foundation. Who belongs to this community becomes clear, especially in 3:33ff.: everyone who hears Jesus' word with faith and does the will of God and thus associates himself with the new spiritual "family" of Jesus.

At the same time, the front of the opponents of Jesus is

declared: they are those who do not want to understand the ministry of Jesus as bound up with God and malevolently suspect him of an alliance with Satan (3:22-30), that is to say, they wish to pervert his divine mission into its opposite. The people too must decide between the two fronts of the disciples of Jesus and his declared enemies. The parable instruction which is presented to the " whole crowd " (4:2) carries out precisely this critical function. As much as the parables are comprehensible on the surface, they disclose their real meaning, the presence of God's reign in the ministry of Jesus, only to the believers who are ready and able to receive God's word, to whom, in the end, God alone discloses his revelation.

The final chapter of this section presents mighty deeds of Jesus, especially great and impressive ones compared with those at the beginning of his mission (4:35—5:43). They occur, however, as far as possible away from the people: the calming of the storm experienced only by his disciples, an extraordinarily difficult exorcism in a lonely region east of the sea, the raising of the daughter of Jairus, into whose house Jesus only takes Peter and the sons of Zebedee, James and John (5:37), and out of which he turns all the others except father and mother (5:40). The " Messiah secret " is still further intensified; Jesus' reserve towards the people (which nevertheless still throng around him, cf. 5:24, 31) becomes more perceptible. Thus it is not surprising that this section ends in a negative occurrence revealing unbelief, namely, the rejection of Jesus in his home town.

The Election of the Twelve; Defense Against Opponents; a Look at Jesus' New Family (3:13-35)

This chapter presents a unity rich in tension: in the beginning the election of the twelve evokes for the reader a picture of the later church underlined by Jesus' purposeful action. With this founding action of Jesus there is sharply contrasted, as a counterpart, the massing together of forces inimical to Jesus. Behind the human antagonists Satan becomes visible with the forces at his disposal, those forces to which his opponents would like to attribute Jesus' successes. Then there follows a scene with the earthly relatives of Jesus which presents the occasion and background to Jesus' words about his spiritual family which is important to the community. One could say that the visible structure of the church, appearing on the horizon, through the election of the twelve, becomes known here also from the inside.

The Election of the Twelve (3:13–19)

[13]*And he went up into the hills, and called to him those he desired; and they came to him.* [14]*And he appointed twelve, to be with him, and to be sent out to preach* [15]*and have authority to cast out demons:* [16]*Simon whom he surnamed Peter;* [17]*James the son of Zebedee and John the brother of James, whom he surnamed Boanerges, that is, sons of thunder,* [18]*Andrew, and Philip and Bartholomew, and Matthew, and Thomas, and James the son of Alphaeus, and Thaddaeus, and Simon the Cananaean,* [19]*and Judas Iscariot, who betrayed him.*

This scene is set apart from the preceding summary account, which gave an account of the powerful throng of people at the Sea of Galilee (v. 7), by the mention of the *hills*. No definite hills are mentioned. The scenic notation has instead a theological significance: Jesus withdraws from the people and seeks the *nearness of God.* The hills are a place of prayer (6:46) to which one climbs up from the lowlands of human ambition to be nearer to God (cf. 9:2). To this place of remoteness from mankind and closeness to God, Jesus takes with him those whom " he desired," those twelve whom he called to himself, that they might be with him and be sent out by him. In Mark the scene is construed differently than in Luke, where Jesus spends the night in prayer and on the morning elects the " twelve " who are also called " apostles " (Lk. 6:12f.) out of a great crowd of disciples. The people, or a greater band of disciples, are not mentioned in Mark. By a free decision, Jesus calls those elected to himself and takes them into God's region, just as he later takes the three disciples closest to him still farther up on a *high* mountain where he is transfigured before them and where they hear God's testimony to his Son (9:2–7).

The *twelve* are in Jesus' intention the representatives of the twelve tribes of *holy Israel,* which he has in mind in its original and eschatological form (the Israel of the day comprised only two-and-a-half tribes, and whom he wants to reach with his message and saving mission (cf. Mt. 10:6; 15:24; 19:28). The choice of precisely twelve men is like a prophetic, symbolic action of Jesus. He lays claim to the people of God, whom he desires to gather and complete. For the Christian reader, these twelve become representatives of the new people of God, the community of Christ which is built on them. Where Mark speaks of the " twelve "—and he does fairly often—the special tone vis-à-vis the crowd, which constituted Jesus' audience at the time, is unmistakable. This is especially clear on the occasion in Capernaum " in the house," when he instructs the twelve after their dispute as to who is the greatest (9:35), which is then elaborated into a kind of " community rule " (9:33–50). It is also clear on the occasion of the third prophecy of the passion, where the " twelve " are taken aside from the crowd and alone receive the detailed description of the things that are going to happen to the " Son of man." The " twelve " more so than the " disciples " are a sign that the future community is being addressed.

In verse 14 the aim of the appointment of these men is out-lined: fellowship with Jesus and participation in his mission. The foundation is their close association with Jesus, a com-munity of life, profession, and fate, which basically mean their reception into Jesus' closeness to God. That is why they go up to the " hills " with Jesus and for that reason too they must first be called by Jesus; fellowship with God and with him whom he sent can only be a gift from God. The freedom of Jesus in " calling to him those he desired " comes from the certainty of knowing and fulfilling the will of God. He knows in his heart that " the secret of the kingdom of God " (4 : 11) has been given to these men by God himself in a revelation through grace. The community of Christ is a supernatural foundation which came into being through freedom and the grace of God. Its life center, its springs of power and the mystery of its being, is its union with Christ and through him with God. The earthly association of the twelve with their master is perpetuated in the spiritual community of the faithful with their heavenly Lord. The order which Jesus imposes on the sharply defined circle of disciples, especially the basic precept of serving love (9 : 33–35; 10 : 35–45), is also valid for the later community of the faithful.

Jesus elects the " twelve," however, for a special task. He wants to send them out, hence to share in his own task. This is made clear in that the purpose of their mission is circumscribed by the same two activities which are characteristic of Jesus' work in Mark: *preaching and casting out demons* (cf. 1:27, 39). The two involve full authority, which is clearly demonstrated in the casting out of demons. The matter rests, to begin with, with the " appointment " of the twelve and a definition of their task; not until later are they sent out to execute their task (6:7-13). It suffices that this circle has been established as a sign of God; just as the mystery of Jesus is not disclosed till the resurrection, so the full significance of Jesus' action cannot be grasped except by the later community, which at the same time finds its own self-knowledge in it.

The evangelist then calls these men by *name*. The arrangement of the list, the sequence of names, and the details added to individual names are revealing. The specifications in Matthew and Luke do not fully tally with this and partly betray personal leanings. Mark not only places Simon at the head of the list (as all the others do), not only emphasizes (stronger than the others) the addition of the symbolic name " Peter," but also isolates this leading disciple from his brother Andrew in order to link him closely, instead, with the sons of Zebedee, James and John. These three then become the privileged witnesses of some events: the awakening of the daughter of Jairus (5:37), the transfiguration of Jesus (9:2), and his agony in Gethsemani (14:33). Considering the link between these events, they become especially capable of grasping the mystery of Jesus' person, his concealed divinity in his earthly ministry, but also his way to the cross and beyond, and then of revealing this to the community. Only Mark notes in this text that Jesus calls the sons of Zebedee the " sons of thunder," an expression whose meaning cannot be explained with certainty. It probably not only refers to their passionate natures (cf. Lk. 9:54) but also contains (like Peter = rock) an effective prophecy: they are exposed to the eschatological thunder storm, to suffer with their Master the baptism of death (cf. 10:38-40)—" companions in a storm," as someone has put it, who must weather eschatological conflicts and sufferings.

After these disciples distinguished with special titles, the names of the others follow and finally that of Judas Iscariot together with the terrible knowledge, echoing through the entire young church and in all its gospels, that it was he *who betrayed him*. This expression strikes a somber note, especially in the Son-of-man theology of Mark (cf. 9:31; 10:33; 14:18, 21, 41f.). That he was one of the twelve elected by Jesus himself remains an obscure mystery (14:18: " one of you will betray me "), but it is ordered, by the evangelist, under the " must " of salvation history as attested by scripture, that the " Son of man " go the way of the cross to which he is destined (8:31; 14:21). Even the church, founded by the twelve, stands under the sign of the *mysterium iniquitas,* the mystery of evil. This is only hinted at here; on the whole, the pericope remains a reassuring scene for the community which is guided by Jesus into the proximity of God, into the light of God's victoriously approaching kingdom.

Jesus Misconstrued and Accused (3:20-30)

[20]*Then he went home; and the crowd came together again, so that they could not even eat.* [21]*And when his relatives heard it, they went out to seize him, for they said," He is beside himself."*

The aim of this passage is to show the misunderstanding, the misjudgment, and *misconstruction of the person of Jesus* on the part of those naturally close to him. His chafing, his zeal for what concerns him make these people think him "mad." In their narrow-mindedness they want to take him home also perhaps because they are worried about the good name of the family. Totally unsuited for psychiatric inferences as to the mental state of Jesus, this text, rather, throws a strong light on the mentality of people who lack every organ for God's unconditional claim. They cannot understand that a man known to them and close to them could be completely filled with God's affairs and fully dedicated to his service. Here the same attitude is recorded as with the inhabitants of Nazareth (6:1–6a), which is unmasked as unbelief. Such blindness is always a danger among relatives and friends of those whom God calls to special service, and a warning against mere "natural" thinking and bourgeois concern about good reputation, health, and business. Jesus stands outside humanly intelligible categories and takes his disciples with him also into the total claim of God.

[22]And the scribes who came down from Jerusalem said, " He is possessed by Beelzebub, and by the prince of demons he casts out demons." [23]And he called them to him, and said to them in parables, " How can Satan cast out Satan? [24]If a kingdom is divided against itself, that kingdom cannot stand. [25]And if a house is divided against itself, that house will not be able to stand. [26]And if Satan has risen against himself and is divided, he cannot stand, but is coming to an end. [27]But no one can enter a strong man's house and plunder his goods, unless he first binds the strong man; then, indeed, he may plunder his house."

Just come down from Jerusalem and suspiciously watching his conduct, the scribes are sharply contrasted with the relatives of Jesus, who are, after all, well intentioned. They sow a seed dangerous for Jesus, saying that *he is possessed* (found only in Mark) and *(in league) with the prince of demons he casts out demons.* According to Jewish thought the demons were under the leadership of a prince of demons called " Beelzebub " (" lord of the dwelling "). The names vary (in Qumran there is reference to the " angel of darkness "), but what is meant is the " ruler of this world " (Jn. 12 : 31), as the sequence shows. The suspicion entails nothing less than that Jesus himself is possessed and brings about his undeniable successes through demonic power. That is an enormous blasphemy since they impute an unholy and unclean spirit (cf. vv. 29f.) to him who casts out demons in the Spirit of God (cf. Mt. 12 : 28), or discredit him with being in league with the devil. Jesus would, then, have come to an agreement with God's adversary in order to do his exorcisms—and would, therefore, be all the more the bondsman of Satan.

The parable about the kingdom and the household clearly refutes the accusation of being in league with the devil. Satan would have to fight against himself or someone like himself, his kingdom would be divided and finally crumble, as would happen to a household divided against itself. Even though the picture of a kingdom of demons under the strategy of Ṣatan strikes us as " mythological," the argument, nevertheless, retains its validity : the power of evil is directed as a unity against God, and whoever forces it back must stand on God's side. Jesus' contemporaries were convinced that Satan was involved in cases of possession. It is more difficult for us (as it already was for the young church) to recognize the activity of the evil one. For the young church, it became a criterion of the " discernment of spirits " whether one accepted her *confession of Jesus* or not (cf. 1 Jn. 4 : 2f.). These slanderous attacks against him are repeated in suspicions against his community; but insofar as the church aspires to do the affairs of Jesus and God, she can repel all attacks.

The next parable, concerning the " strong man " guarding his house, is peculiar since the man seems to have right on his side, and yet the *strong man* who is overpowered by the *stronger* could only be Satan. Jesus did not shy away from such " daring " parables in which doubtful occurrences are used (such as the overpowering of the proprietor of a house) to illustrate good ideas. It is a parable in which only one point of comparison is of interest: here a stronger man is at work. From the context, *only Jesus* could be meant here. Further metaphors (like the " house " which the stronger enters, or the " goods " which he plunders) should not be interpreted. There is no doubt about Jesus' awareness of being superior to Satan and being able to overpower him with God's might. Thus this parable becomes an impressive testimony to Jesus' own understanding of his ministry for which the reader is already prepared by the story of the temptation.

Jesus does not thereby characterize himself as the " Messiah " in the Jewish sense, but certainly the possessor and steward of divine powers. Here it becomes clear also that his ministry cannot be separated from his person. It is *he* through whom the casting out of demons occurs, through *him* God's kingdom comes to man (cf. Lk. 11:20), in *his* ministry Satan is overpowered (cf. Lk. 10:18). But all the power of Jesus reveals only the salvation of God; he has always opposed the exercise of earthly power and repelled it as a temptation.

[28]" *Truly, I say to you, all sins will be forgiven the sons of men, and whatever blasphemies they utter;* [29]*but whoever blasphemes*

against the Holy Spirit never has forgiveness, but is guilty of an eternal sin"—[30]*for they had said, " He has an unclean spirit."*

These words about " blasphemy " fit into the context of Mark's form of presentation. *Blasphemy* in the biblical sense means an attack against God's honor and power, directly or indirectly (through an abuse of God-sent men or deeds accomplished by God) and is therefore always a terrible sin. But Jesus assures us that all sins will be forgiven the sons of men, also all blasphemies, except those against the Holy Spirit. Just as liberating as the first part of the declaration sounds, so disturbing does the second. Are there, therefore, " unforgivable " sins? But to interpret the antecedent properly one must add : God will not, in the end, generously forgive all sins without further ado, but only when the sinner is converted to him. The demand for *conversion* (cf. 1 : 4 and 1 : 15) was self-evident to Judaism, and Jesus, too, has often enough stated this condition. When a sinner is converted, turns back to God, the heavenly Father is ready, according to Jesus' teaching, to forgive the greatest guilt (cf. Mt. 18 : 23–25).

But why will a " blasphemy against the Holy Spirit " never be forgiven? In the light of the demand for conversion, the answer to this can only be : because such people persist in an attitude contrary to conversion and harden themselves in it to such an extent that God cannot forgive them. A *sin against the Holy Spirit* is not simply one act, but a persistent attitude of soul, that is to say, a blindness through one's own fault, a struggle against the saving action of God. Insofar as, and as long as, a man persists in his stubborn *contradiction of God* he excludes himself from salvation. This happens when someone ascribes the recognizable effects of God's Spirit in Jesus to the spirit of Satan. Thus the young church, or Mark (cf. v. 30), must have understood that malicious attack on Jesus. These words bring one up against the obscure mystery of a " hardness of heart " (cf. 4:12). Whether people can find a way out of such a thoroughly wrong attitude is not stated here or anywhere else; only to the anxious question of the disciples: " Then who can be saved?" Jesus has answered, what is impossible with men is not impossible with God (10:27). These really serious words about the " unforgivable sin " do not cancel out his message of the boundless mercy of God, but they show the converse and the consequence for those men who willfully shut their minds to the invitation to be converted and saved, and persist in the contradiction of the One sent by God and of the Holy Spirit at work in him.

The New Family of Jesus (3:31–35)

[31]*And his mother and his brethren came; and standing outside they sent to him and called him.* [32]*And a crowd was sitting about him; and they said to him, " Your mother and your brethren are outside asking for you." * [33]*And he replied, " Who are my mother and my brethren?" * [34]*And looking around at those who sat about him, he said, " Here are my mother and my brethren! * [35]*Whoever does the will of God is my brother, and sister, and mother."*

The evangelist still holds on to the scene of Jesus in the " home " with a great crowd about him (v. 20). After the dismissal of his opponents, Jesus now also dismisses his immediate relatives, but in a totally different sense. The mother and " brethren " of Jesus, that is to say, cousins, according to several manuscripts, want to visit him; that is something different from the intention of his " relatives " in verse 21 to seize him (see above). The close relatives of Jesus have come to Capernaum from Nazareth, but they remain in front of the door in view of the crowd and let Jesus be called out. We do not hear of a negative attitude towards them. Jesus has left them in order to follow the call of God and now he demonstrates that he has also freed himself internally from them, not from coldness or contempt of the family bonds (which are very strong in Palestine) but in order to *belong to God* totally. What he demands of his *disciples* (cf. Mt. 10:37) he has done himself. However, his answer has not only this exemplary significance, above all it concerns the self-understanding of the community.

Instead of the earthly family, Jesus has chosen another, the *spiritual family*. He looks at the people who sit around him and calls them his " mother and brethren." Mark often speaks of such " looking around " on the part of Jesus (3:5; 5:37; 10:23; 11:11). His look betrays inner wakefulness and attention but also draws attention to special ideas. Related to this passage is his looking around at his disciples after the departure of the " rich youth " (10:23). A word follows which makes them think. Does Jesus only want to affirm that those there are his true relaives, because they are listening to his words? In that case this scene would be closely related to the other in the house of the two sisters, Martha and Mary, where listening to Jesus' word is praised and recommended (Lk. 10:39–42). But there is no explicit reference here to " listening to his word," although it is undoubtedly presupposed. Instead Jesus continues: " whoever does the will of God is my brother, and sister, and mother." This makes the scene closer still to another where Jesus corrects a woman's cry of praise from the crowd with the words:

" Blessed rather are those who hear the word of God and keep it " (Lk. 11:27f.). It is, therefore, more a *challenge* to those sitting there and to the later community to join in a spiritual fellowship with Jesus by doing the will of God. In that way, the content of the declaration is unfolded for the later community: it is conscious of being the crowd gathered " around Jesus," listening to his word. Still more, it keeps his word, in order to do completely and exclusively God's will. Vocation and challenge, election and demand, joyful bonds and demanding responsibility: all this is implied. And this unity of tensions is what, first of all, determines the consciousness of the " family " of Jesus, the eschatological people of God.

Teaching in Parables (4:1–34)

The community of God is to come together by rallying around Jesus listening to his words, and fulfilling the will of God. But that is a process which in view of Jesus' own experience is surrounded by a deep mystery. Many people throng to him, and yet only a few grasp what is happening: the dawning of God's kingdom in this world, the fulfilled time of salvation in the ministry of Jesus. Most people remain " outside," outside a believing understanding, outside, too, of the true community of belief which lives for the knowledge of the presence of salvation. When Jesus " teaches " people, these are not only " teachings " to be pondered, but it is an occurrence which brings about a division into those who listen merely with their ears and those who listen with faith, those who are blind and those who understand, those who are hard of heart and those who are open to the call of God.

This chapter in Mark's gospel, the longest discursive passage in the public ministry of Jesus, surely also aims at presenting the main content of the preaching of Jesus, the message of the approaching kingdom of God (cf. 1 : 15). It does not, however, simply record the historical " teaching of Jesus " but intends also to highlight its impact on the people of the day, its significance for the circle of disciples, and above all its importance for the later community.

The Parable of the Sower (4 :1–9)

[1]*Again he began to teach beside the sea. And a very large crowd gathered about him, so that he got into a boat and sat in it on the sea; and the whole crowd was beside the sea on the land.* [2]*And he taught them many things in parables, and in his teaching he said to them:* [3]*" Listen! A sower went out to sow.* [4]*And as he sowed, some seed fell along the path, and the birds came and devoured it.* [5]*Other seed fell on rocky ground, where it had not much soil, and immediately it sprang up, since it had no depth of soil;* [6]*and when the sun rose it was scorched, and since it had no root it withered away.* [7]*Other seed fell among thorns and the thorns grew up and choked it, and it yielded no grain.* [8]*And other seed fell into good soil and brought forth grain, growing up and increasing and yielding thirtyfold and sixtyfold and a hundredfold."* [9]*And he said, " He who has ears to hear let him hear."*

Let us, to begin with, leave aside the strongly allegorical and moral interpretation of the young church which is later offered to the disciples (vv. 14–20). Jesus tells of an *everyday occurrence:* a farmer walks over the poor, stony ground of the Galilean hill country and sows there the seeds of corn. In doing this, much seed is lost by falling either on the path, on rocky ground, or among thorns. Only a small part (the four examples illustrate this) finds good soil, but it yields abundant, overabundant fruit. In those days in Palestine one did not plough the earth until after the sowing, hence the seed was ploughed into the ground. This explains the depicted fate of the seed. What Jesus is relating, therefore, is nothing unusual. He wants to illustrate for his audience a deeper *spiritual occurrence* by using a process of human life and nature familiar to them. It must be something connected with the kingdom of God. At least, that is how the evangelist understands it, for he sees the significant nucleus in the words: " To you has been given the secret of the kingdom of God " (v. 11). The other parables also speak with increasing clarity of the kingdom of God (cf. vv. 26 and 30). But what is the special meaning of this parable with reference to the message of the kingdom of God?

Let us proceed from what is certain. By the " secret of the kingdom of God " Jesus could only have meant its *presence in his ministry*. Thus the parable describes something that is in the process of happening. The reader knows this from the account so far: the kingdom of God is being proclaimed, its might becomes tangible in word and deed; but it also meets opposition, the power of Satan and the suspicions of men (cf. 3:20–30). As Jesus tells the story of the sower and his seed, the attention of the audience is directed towards the fate of the seed. The details as to how and why so much seed is lost are hardly important. The first three groups depict only the fact that so much is sown in vain; but this failure is compensated for by the abundant fruit of the last group. Even as a narrative, all the emphasis lies on this *harvest*. The parable ends with it, giving glad assurance. This is what Jesus seems to be aiming at: to give the certainty that the proclamation will be successful in spite of all opposition, that the beginning promises fulfillment.

Does Jesus regard himself to be the " sower "? If so, then only very reservedly; in the parable the sower is mentioned only in the beginning, the focus is entirely on *the seed*. That corresponds to the *proclamation of Jesus,* who with his words and deeds only wishes to bring God's message of salvation and to illustrate God's dealings. Of course, the sowing is done by him; but the parable remains open also for later proclaimers who take up his activity. The young church understands that Jesus' proclamation of the gospel lives on in her own missionary preaching (cf. v. 14, " the word ").

The word of God is mighty and fruitful, the advance of God's kingdom cannot be resisted. While it is being proclaimed it is offered to man. He need only *hear* and *believe*. Thus there is also a mighty appeal in this parable to be receptive to the word of salvation, here and now in the time of sowing. The final word, added with a new start, must have been an oft-repeated admonition of Jesus, but here too it is very much to the point: " He who has ears to hear let him hear." Correct hearing is not what the parable teaches, but it discloses the meaning of the parable: to cultivate confidence in the proclaimed kingdom of God and its power, hope in its consummation and its coming in glory.

The Reason for Speaking in Parables (4:10-12)

[10]*And when he was alone, those who were about him with the twelve asked him concerning the parables.* [11]*And he said to them, " To you has been given the secret of the kingdom of God, but*

for those outside everything is a riddle; [12]*so that they may indeed
see but not perceive, and may indeed hear but not understand;
lest they should turn again and be forgiven."*

This intermediary passage, which, as a special piece of instruction, is addressed only to those close to Jesus, considers speaking
in parables as such and inquires into the reason for it. Although
Jesus has so far told only *one* parable, they ask him about *the*
parables, that is, about the meaning which they have as a whole
and, with this, the reason why he uses the parable form of speech
(cf. Mt. 13:10). Clearly, it is the *later community* which is
inquiring here, just as in other instances where Jesus gives
" private " instruction to his disciples it is for the purpose of
interpreting the words of Jesus for the community (cf. 4:34;
7:37; 9:28, 33; 10:10; 13:3). This also explains the vague
form of speech: " those who were about him with the twelve."
In other instances it is the twelve who receive more detailed
explanations of this kind; but " those who were about him "
are mentioned especially because they represent the later believers
—in contrast to " those outside " (v. 11). The horizon is extended
beyond the narrow circle of disciples to all who belong to Jesus
(cf. 3:34f.).

The word itself which the evangelist uses in reference to the
" parables " had probably originally a more comprehensive
meaning. " Everything " is for those outside a " riddle," that is,
turns into difficult and unintelligible questions. The word can
have this meaning too. Jesus' entire preaching, indeed, including
his entire ministry, becomes for *those outside* a riddle, because
they cannot see it and understand it with believing eyes. The
" secret " which corresponds to this " riddle " can unveil itself
or remain veiled.

The *secret of the kingdom of God* which is " given " to the believing disciples refers to their closeness to Jesus in his ministry. God's kingdom is already a fact; the seed is being sown, the powers are at work. In Jesus' words and actions the new is already tangible; what is being proclaimed is already happening: healing as a sign of salvation, casting out of demons as a proof of divine might, forgiveness of sins as an expression of divine mercy. Those who have eyes of faith can see all this (cf. Lk. 10:23ff.; Mt. 13:16f.). We are reminded of another pronouncement of Jesus, namely, the " cry of joy ": " I thank thee, Father, Lord of heaven and earth, that thou hast hidden these things from the wise and understanding and revealed them to babes " (Mt. 11:25 = Lk. 10:21). Here again two groups of people are contrasted: the humanly wise and understanding to whom it remains hidden, and the " babes," that is to say, the *humble and uneducated* to whom it is innerly revealed by God himself. Only with " simple " faith can one grasp the secret of God's kingdom.

In fact only a few people have grasped this secret. This *knowledge* is at the root of those harsh words of Jesus. The " outsiders " for whom the entire ministry of Jesus has become a " riddle " are all unbelievers lacking in understanding. This also includes, for the later community, those who shut their minds to its missionary preaching. That God's call remains without any response in the case of so many people is for believers a dark, depressing fact which can only be mastered in the light of the divine plan for salvation, in the light of scripture. The quotation, a passage from the sixth chapter of the Book of Isaiah, the vision referring to the prophet's vocation, has occupied the young church in other places also. Luke refers to it at the end of the Acts (28:26f.). After a long endeavor to convert the Jewish people, John refers to it in his review of the public ministry of Jesus (12:40). According to Mark, the exclusion of the outsiders happens intentionally, "that they may indeed see but do not perceive . . ." It sounds like a terrible *hardness of heart* willed by God. We are, however, dealing with a quotation; Jesus is referring to the will of God as expressed in scripture. We must, therefore, consider the quotation in the light of the circumstances which that passage presupposes. When the prophet was called by God, the people had turned away from him and the prophet has to announce to these refractory people the punishment of God: it is to remain hard and deceived to its destruction; only a holy remainder is to survive. Thus the hardness of heart is not without guilt for those whose minds remain shut to Jesus' preaching (cf. Mt. 13:13: " because seeing they do not see "), and perhaps it is only a temporal punishment (cf. Rom. 11:7ff.). Even so, God's salvific counsel remains hard enough; but it is not unintelligible in the economy of salvation history.

Explanation and Application of the Parable of the Sower (4:13–20

[13]*And he said to them, " Do you not understand this parable? How then will you understand all the parables? *[14]*The sower sows the word. *[15]*And these are the ones along the path, where the word is sown; when they hear, Satan immediately comes and takes away the word that is sown in them. *[16]*And these in like manner are the ones sown on rocky ground, who, when they hear the word, immediately receive it with joy; *[17]*and they have no root in themselves, but endure for a while; then when tribulation or persecution arises on account of the word, immediately they fall away. *[18]*And others are the ones sown among thorns;*

they are those who hear the word, [19]*but the cares of the world,
the delight in riches and the desire for other things, enter in and
choke the word, and it proves unfruitful.* [20]*But those that were
sown upon good soil are the ones who hear the word and accept
it and bear fruit, thirtyfold and sixtyfold and a hundredfold.*

This explanation of the parable of the sower given to the disciples
is in reality an *application of the young church* to those converted to the faith and their situation in the world. This is
clearly recognizable from the linguistic formulation and the presupposed conditions (tribulation and persecution, seduction of
the world). The original viewpoint (sowing and harvest) has
been peculiarly shifted to the people addressed: they are now
the " sown," put into the conditions of this world. They are
also the " ground " on which the word is sown (v. 15). The
figurative bluntness, the fusion of two metaphors, results from
the attempt to speak forcefully to the hearers and admonish them
to bear fruit.

The parenesis is impressive. Those "along the path," from
whom Satan takes away the seed of the word, can be interpreted as those who are robbed of their germinating faith by
enemies of the faith. Others find the reason for their falling away
in themselves: they have no depth and constancy (stony ground).
For the moment they are enthusiastic, but in times of persecution
and tribulation they do not persevere in the faith. They have not
understood the meaning of the religion of the cross, the call to
imitation. Then there are those deceptive desires which " choke "
the inner life. The " cares of the world," the struggle for a
livelihood, the privations and the disappointments in life are
just as stifling as riches and instinctual desires. Prosperity makes
man satiated, self-satisfied, deceives him as to his true condition,

and makes him forget God and his true salvation (cf. Lk. 12:
16–20, the rich corn farmer). But the exposition does not stop
at this negative and depressing approach. God has not sown
his seed in vain. Where his word falls on good soil it brings forth
manifold fruit, extremely rich fruit. This is an encouraging
appeal to all those converted to the faith and, at the same time,
a consolation in face of the failure and falling away of many.
God's word does not return to him empty without having first
accomplished what he intends and prospered in the thing for
which it was sent (Is. 55:8–11).

The missionary framework (" the sower sows the word ") also
suggests another application. Christian *missionaries,* who take on
and continue Christ's work of sowing, receive *insight and consolation* for their ministry. Failures are not excluded. In the
parable three parts of the seed are lost, only a quarter falls on
good ground. This is certainly not meant to be mathematical, but
it hints at the mystery of God's economy. God achieves his aim
against much opposition, and in the end he harvests a rich fruit.
He works by different rules than mankind; there is a paradox
of divine strength in weakness (cf. 1 Cor. 1:25).

A Group of Sayings (4:21–25)

²¹*And he said to them, " Is a lamp brought in to be put under a
bushel, or under a bed, and not on a stand? ²²For there is nothing
hid, except to be made manifest; nor is anything secret, except
to come to light. ²³If any man has ears to hear let him hear."
²⁴And he said to them, " Take heed what you hear; the measure
you give will be the measure you get, and still more will be given
to you. ²⁵For to him who has will more be given; and for him
who has not, even what he has will be taken away."*

The easily comprehensible image of the *lamp* which should be on a stand refers to the proclamation of God's kingdom. Jesus too has preached and taught in public, but the majority of people remained in incomprehension and unbelief. Only the narrower circle of his disciples accepted his words in faith, and God disclosed to them the " secret of the kingdom of God." But the gospel has to be preached to the whole world (13:10; 14:9); the disciples must carry this light into the world. In the proclaimed word the kingdom of God becomes effective and present. Faith must have missionary energy. A community which confines itself to its own circle is like someone who puts a lamp under a bushel or a bed. If in the ministry of Jesus it was the will of God to confide the mystery of the kingdom of God to only a few, and if the preaching of Jesus was intended only for the people of Israel to begin with, the gospel must, nonetheless, be proclaimed at some time to all nations (13:10). It is the light which is to shine for *all mankind*.

Thus the following saying, which speaks of things hid and secret which are to be made manifest, is well aligned. This general remark is here applied to the event of proclaiming the word itself. Mark is emphasizing the inner meaning and direction of this event which is now hidden; what is now hidden shall be revealed, what is now secret shall be made known. Also the secret of the person and ministry of Jesus, the secret of God's kingdom, are to be made manifest to mankind after Easter. There is a strong exhortation here to the preachers of the word and the community, which is reinforced by the challenge: " If someone has ears to hear let him hear." The whole community is to become keen of hearing and to grasp the task of *ministry in the world*. To lead a hidden life is contrary to the will of God. The church must never retreat into a ghetto or become a petty sect. She must be a sign of God in the world and give witness to God's work (cf. Mt. 5 : 13–16).

The proper type of hearing is also important. The focus now turns from the proclaimers to the hearers: " Take heed what you hear." In this context the saying about the measure means the measure of readiness to receive. Certainly, the image fits better into the admonition against condemning one's brother (Mt. 7 : 1) or the advice to give generously (Lk. 6 : 38); but the addition by Mark, " and still more will be given to you " (v. 24), indicates how the evangelist understood it: he who *makes room* for God's word and lets it unfold will have a *rich gain*. One must accept the message of God with a ready heart and open one's heart wide to it that it bear fruit. " Let the word of Christ dwell in you richly " (Col. 3 : 16). Hearing does not mean merely a receptive behavior but demands a personal participation, the will to assimilate what is heard and to make it fruitful in one's own life. He who takes heed of what is preached to him and " measures " it as God's revelation and as a challenge to himself will draw benefit and increasing profit from it. God himself will increase the treasure of his faith and delight him with inner gifts.

The Parable of the Seed Growing by Itself (4 :26–29)

[26]*And he said, " The kingdom of God is as if a man should scatter seed upon the ground,* [27]*and should sleep and rise night and day, and the seed should sprout and grow, he knows not how.* [28]*The earth produces of itself, first the blade, then the ear, then the full grain in the ear.* [29]*But when the grain is ripe, at once he puts in the sickle, because the harvest has come."*

Now the evangelist tells a second kingdom-of-God parable

which is again about seed, growth, and harvest. It is preserved
only by Mark. Luke is satisfied with the parable of the sower
and sayings linked with it; Matthew presents, in this place, the
parable of the weed among the wheat, not without a purpose,
surely. Mark wishes to clarify the message of Jesus about the
approaching kingdom of God. He directs his gaze now to the
time in between sowing and the harvest. One could say that in
the three parables of Mark 4, the accent is shifted from the sowing (parable of the sower) to the in-between-time (growing seed)
and from there to the end (the mustard seed). But all three
aspects are present each time; seed, growth, and harvest cannot
be separated from one another.

The parable tells of a self-evident process known to all the
listeners and disputed by none. But Jesus wants to teach something definite about the kingdom of God and exhorts his
listeners to a behavior corresponding to God's action at the
moment. But what is the *special appeal* of the parable? After
the sowing of the seed the farmer waits patiently and calmly
until the time of harvest has come. The earth produces of itself.
The harvest will certainly come and then the farmer can immediately bring in his crop.

In spite of all the calm waiting, the focus is, nonetheless, on
the *harvest*. When the grain is ripe the farmer puts in his sickle.
The last words are a quotation from Joel 4:13 and have their
chief stress in the joyful exclamation: " The harvest has come."
Thus the community is exhorted to keep itself prepared for
God's harvest at the end of time.

In his time, Jesus wished to reinforce confidence in God and in
his work: God's kingdom is certainly coming and is near at
hand. It comes through God's power and grows quietly " of
itself " without one noticing it. This thought becomes actual in

a new way in the post-Easter time of the community. The community, already developing a missionary dissemination of the word but besieged by failure and difficulties, is exhorted to remain calm and confident, patient and steadfast, leaving further development to God while it directs its gaze to the future. The expectation which filled the community (cf. 9:1; 13:30), supported by the parable of the figtree (13:28f.), that the kingdom of God will be there soon is thereby put into proper perspective: it is not a temporal proximity of the kingdom that is decisive; rather, it is the *ever effective proximity* of God who knows the day and the hour (13:32). The parable requires a similar basic attitude from us: a believing confidence in God who works quietly and allows his seed to ripen, and a calmness which draws peace and strength from this knowledge.

The Parable of the Mustard Seed (4:30–34)

[30]*And he said, " With what can we compare the kingdom of God, or what parable shall we use for it? *[31]*It is like a grain of mustard seed, which, when sown upon the ground, is the smallest of all the seeds on earth; *[32]*yet when it is sown it grows up and becomes the greatest of all shrubs, and puts forth large branches, so that the birds of the air can make nests in its shade." *[33]*With many such parables he spoke the word to them, as they were able to hear it; *[34]*he did not speak to them without a parable, but privately to his own disciples he explained everything.*

The last of these parables begins with a cumbersome introduction. The double question could indicate how difficult it is to make clear to the listeners the truth and reality of the kingdom of God. As always with these parables, the kingdom of God should not be simply equated with the selected metaphor (here the mustard seed). It is, rather, illustrated by the process as a whole. From the small mustard seed grows the powerful shrub. That is an astonishing process. This growth from the smallest beginnings to the greatest development is what the parable is meant to convey. The proverbially small mustard seed (cf. Lk. 17:6=Mt. 17:20) has the power within itself to grow into a great plant and to put out large branches in whose shade the birds make nests. The individual steps in the growth are not described here as in the parable of the self-growing seed. Rather, the focus is on the impressive *final result*. The parable of the yeast is not intended to illustrate anything different, and it certainly must have originally been joined to the parable of the mustard seed as a double parable (Lk. 13:18–21; Mt. 13:31–33). The glory of the final event is also indicated by the " birds of the air," an image already known from the Old Testament. The dwelling of the birds in the shadow or the branches of the tree is like a symbol of the kingdom of God: it encompasses many peoples and becomes a home for them.

This parable ought not immediately to remind us of the growth and spread of the *church*. God's kingdom is, indeed, effective on earth and in the church, but it has no visible dimension and is not a solid institution like the church. It is not subject to earthly development, as the church is in the course of its history. It does not develop through natural factors, through the planning and dealings of men. It grows, rather, through God's hidden power. Thus the double parable of the mustard seed and the yeast does not illustrate the extensive and intensive accomplishments of the church. It assures us instead that the cosmic kingdom of God is coming. The thought of the triumphant expansion of the church or our ability " to build up the kingdom of God " is a dangerous deception which is also refuted by earthly history. Jesus is only thinking of God's wonderful powers and God's indisputable final success.

From this viewpoint of revelation, the parable of the mustard seed is a powerful incentive to an unshakable *faith* and unerring *hope*. Contrary to all outward appearances, the kingdom of God will develop and be victorious in the end. That is what the evangelist wishes to convey to his community. In spite of his strong missionary interests, he does not fall into the temptation of harboring worldly hopes for the future. He knows, indeed, that the gospel must be *proclaimed* to all nations before the end (13:10). But he also knows that before the coming of the Son of man there will be much persecution, seduction, and great tribulation (13:5-23). This focus on the final victory of God is also very significant for us.

Great Deeds of Power and Rejection at Nazareth (4:35—6:6a)

Jesus' message and teaching are confirmed by his great miracles, not in the sense of a " proof " that the powers of God's kingdom are in him, but in the sense of signs which illustrate these powers—for all who see them with believing eyes. What John, the fourth evangelist, later expressly elucidates by his concept of " signs " and by his symbolically profound exposition of the great deeds of Jesus is indirectly hinted at in Mark's presentation. The believing community, who has understood the teaching of Jesus, the " secret of God's kingdom," in parables, now receives a visual lesson of how in Jesus' ministry God's power of salvation is con-

cealed and yet visibly breaking through. God's kingdom was proclaimed from the beginning and, at the same time, was seen to
be presently effective, especially in the casting out of demons
(cf. 1:27, 39; 3:15). One cannot overlook the close relationship
between the deeds of power in the following accounts and the
casting out of demons (1:23-27, 34; 3:11) and the healings
(1:29-31, 40-45; 3:10) related earlier. The calming of the storm
(4:35-41) is depicted as a cosmic exorcism of demons in nature.
The Gerasene demoniac (5:1-20) is a magnified case of the
breaking of demonic powers. The woman with a haemorrhage
(5:25-34) gives an example of the "power that had gone out
from him" (5:30) and which becomes efficacious even by touch
alone (cf. 3:10). Finally, the raising to life of the daughter of
Jairus (5:35-43) is a great, in this context the greatest, sign of
Jesus' life-giving power, snatching mankind even from the
kingdom of death. Jesus makes visible the power of God in his
victory over the demons and the salvation of God in his healings.

But in order to see and understand the significance of the
saving power of God revealed in Jesus, *faith* is necessary. This
theme that faith is adjoined to the self-revelation of Jesus in
mighty deeds becomes more prominent than ever in this section.
In the storm at sea the disciples, and with them the later community, receive a serious lesson on the necessity of faith and a
picture of what faith means in this godless world. The woman
with the hemorrhage becomes a shining example of a faith which
is strong and simple. In the face of death, Jesus exhorts the father
of the girl: "Do not fear, only believe" (5:36). Unbelieving
people, however, fear the revealed power of God and urge Jesus
to depart (5:17), or even laugh at him (5:40). The bitterest
example of unbelief is found at the end: the unbelieving home-
town of Jesus rejects him; he could not do a single mighty deed

there, and he marveled at their unbelief (6:5f.). That is an
unmistakable warning to anyone who stands close to Jesus and
professes to know him.

The Calming of the Storm (4:35–41)

*35On that day, when the evening had come, he said to them,
" Let us go across to the other side." 36And leaving the crowd,
they took him with them just as he was in the boat. And other
boats were with him. 37And a great storm of wind arose, and the
waves beat into the boat, so that the boat was already filling.
38But he was in the stern, asleep on the cushion; and they woke
him and said to him, " Teacher, do you not care if we perish?"
39And he awoke and rebuked the wind, and said to the sea,
" Peace! Be still!" And the wind ceased, and there was a great
calm. 40He said to them, " Why are you afraid? Have you no
faith?" 41And they were filled with awe and said to one another,
" Who then is this, that even wind and sea obey him?"*

The power of Jesus, experienced here, is only comprehensible in
the sense intended by the evangelist if, with him, one understands
the adjuration of the storm and the word of command to the sea
as a *casting out of demons*. The Greek word which is used for
" rebuke," or forceful reprimand of the wind, is also to be found
in the adjuration of the demons (1:25 and 9:25). A distinction is
evidently made in Mark between the demons of storms and sea
(not so in Matthew or Luke). Every word of command corresponds to a definite result: " The wind ceased and the sea became
calm," two marvelous happenings since the waves normally do
not become calm so quickly. The " natural " explanation that
such violent storms suddenly arise on the sea of Galilee and just

as quickly die down breaks down, however, in face of the experienced fishermen among Jesus' disciples who must have known about this. The portrayal echoes a special experience: first, fear of death (v. 38), then after the sudden calm another type of " fear," awe before him who accomplished this with a short word of command. Even the description of the disciples' reaction is similar to that of the people after the first exorcism (1 : 27). Jesus' power over the wind and the sea proves him to be master over demonic powers.

That the powers of God are present in Jesus cannot be deduced from his outward appearance. He behaves wholly like a man : after the tiring day of preaching at the sea before great crowds of people, he sleeps on the hard cushion where normally the helmsman sits, and not even the noise of the storm and the waves beating against the boat wake him. The disciples wake him, but then he acts immediately and in a manner which is without parallel. The motif of rescue from peril at sea is old (the Jonah story, also Jewish and pagan stories); but in other incidents God is the rescuer or it is the prayer of the pious which brings down help. Here someone acts in God's name and utters only a word of command. *Who is this?* The full authority of Jesus is unique, but it is in a certain sense hidden and reveals itself only in " secret epiphanies."

The whole incident is at the same time an experience of the disciples and a lesson for them. In Matthew the last words of astonishment are spoken by the " men." In Mark it is always the disciples. Danger of death made them forget who they had in their midst; the powers to which they saw themselves exposed overpowered their faith. This is openly expressed in Jesus' words of reproach : they are *fearful and cowardly*. Again it is Mark who with his double question brings this out more forcefully than any other evangelist. For him, the disciples completely lost faith, whereas Matthew speaks of " men of little faith." Faith is here not yet a reflective faith in Jesus, the Christ and Son of God. It is the elementary force of believing confidence. It must survive all the assaults of powers hostile to God. It is the prerequisite for the understanding of Jesus' message about God's kingdom. The last question, however, gives the reader also to understand that it must be a faith in Jesus the Son of God.

The Healing of the Gerasene Demoniac (5 :1–20)

¹They came to the other side of the sea, to the country of the Gerasenes. ²And when he had come out of the boat, there met him out of the tombs a man with an unclean spirit, ³who lived among the tombs; and no one could bind him any more even with a chain; ⁴for he had often been bound with fetters and chains, but the chains he wrenched apart, and the fetters he broke in pieces; and no one had the strength to subdue him. ⁵Night and day among the tombs and on the mountains he was always crying out, and bruising himself with stones. ⁶And when he saw Jesus from afar, he ran and worshiped him; ⁷and crying out with a loud voice, he said, " What have you to do with me, Jesus, Son of the Most High God? I adjure you by God, do not torment me." ⁸For he had said to him, " Come out of the man you unclean spirit!" ⁹And Jesus asked him, " What is your name? " He replied, " My name is Legion; for we are many." ¹⁰And he begged him eagerly not to send him out of the country. ¹¹Now a great herd of swine was feeding there on the hillside; ¹²and they begged him, " Send us to the swine, let us enter them." ¹³So he gave them leave. And the unclean spirits came out, and entered the swine, and the herd numbering about two thousand, rushed down the steep bank into the sea, and were drowned in the sea. [14]The herdsmen fled and told it in the city and in the country. And the people came to see what it was that had happened. [15]And they came to Jesus, and saw the demoniac sitting there, clothed and in his right mind, the man who had had the legion; and they were afraid. [16]And those who had seen it told what had happened to the demoniac and to the swine. [17]And they began to beg Jesus to depart from their neighborhood. [18]And as he was getting into the boat, the man who had been possessed with demons begged him that he might go with him. [19]But he refused, and said to him, " Go home to your friends, and tell them how much the Lord has done for you, and how he has had mercy on you." [20]And he went away and began to proclaim in the Decapolis how much Jesus had done for him; and all men marveled.

This story, which strikes us as remarkable, makes good sense in the presentation of the evangelist, except for features which betray the popular notions of that time. It leads to a climax of Jesus' ministry in *divine power*. It deals with an unusually difficult case of possession. The man is raving mad and cannot be subdued even by strong fetters. His horrible sojourn among the tombs on the mountains—according to the notions of the time, a place favored by unclean spirits—his loud cries on the mountains which can be heard day and night down as far as the villages and farms, his wild demeanor: all this underlines the seriousness of the case.

But Jesus also frees this poor man from his tormentors. After the healing he sits there dressed and in his right mind, and that has its impact on the people who know him. It is so unusual that *they are afraid,* that is to say, they tremble at the sight of Jesus' power (v. 15). That is the kernel of the story. The place names indicate the eastern shore, the " Decapolis," which is the area of the hellenistic " confederation of ten cities " with a mainly pagan population. The cities Gerasa and Gedara (according to another version) do not come into question because they are too far inland. They are surely named only because they are the best-known places of the Decapolis. Origen alleges that a place which sounds like that, namely, Gergesa, was situated on the sea. From the Talmud we know of a place called Kursa, and its name lives on in the Kursi ruins of today, a place where the mountains are close to the sea and decline steeply downwards. There the incident reported here could have taken place.

The end of the story demands greater attention. The healed man expresses the desire to remain with Jesus; but Jesus refuses and sends him to his relatives instead. The healed man is to tell them what the Lord (God) has done for him and how he has had mercy on him. The man, however, does not keep to his commission, but proclaims in the Decapolis, that is, in the entire extensive area, what Jesus has done for him, and they were all amazed (vv. 19f.). Jesus wanted to distract attention from his person and remind the man about *God's* help; but he speaks about Jesus' deed. The healed man was only supposed to tell his relatives about it; but he " proclaimed " in the entire region and thereby becomes a messenger of the gospel.

The Healing of the Woman with a Hemorrhage and the Raising of the Daughter of Jairus (5:21–43)

The following long section (5 : 21–43) shows Jesus as extraordinary healer of the sick and raiser from the dead. In the evangelist's composition two miracles are linked together, the healing of the woman with the hemorrhage and the raising of the daughter of Jairus. Mark begins with the request of the ruler of the synagogue to make his daughter well again by the laying on of hands. Jesus follows him. To begin with, another great miracle occurs on the way. A woman, who touched him in the crowd, is healed of a hemorrhage. The interruption which this causes to the story serves to prepare us for a new phase: the daughter of the ruler of the synagogue has meanwhile died and Jesus meets with loud lamentation at the house. Thus the healing of the sick turns into a raising from the dead, a climax to his ministry as giver of life. The evangelist has consciously led his narrative up to this point. One need not suppose that the woman with the hemorrhage was healed precisely on this occasion; it is the art of the narrator to heighten the tension and lead up to a new climax. The two miracles, however, are painted in such original and fresh colors that one cannot doubt their good tradition.

[21]And when Jesus had crossed again in the boat to the other side, a great crowd gathered around him; and he was beside the sea. [22]Then came one of the rulers of the synagogue, Jairus by name; and seeing him, he fell at his feet, [23]and besought him, saying, " My little daughter is at the point of death. Come and lay your hands on her, so that she may be made well, and live." [24]And he went with him.

And a great crowd followed him and thronged about him. [25]And there was a woman who had had a flow of blood for twelve years, [26]and who had suffered much under many physicians, and had spent all that she had, and was no better but rather grew worse. [27]She had heard the reports about Jesus, and came up behind him in the crowd and touched his garment. [28]For she said, " If I touch even his garments, I shall be made *well." ²⁹And immediately the hemorrhage ceased; and she felt in her body that she was healed of her disease. ³⁰And Jesus, perceiving in himself that power had gone forth from him, immediately turned about in the crowd, and said, " Who touched my garments?" ³¹And his disciples said to him, " You see the crowd pressing around you, and yet you say, ' Who touched me?' " ³²And he looked around to see who had done it. ³³But the woman, knowing what had been done to her, came in fear and trembling and fell down before him, and told the whole truth. ³⁴And he said to her, " Daughter, your faith has made you well; go in peace, and be healed of your disease."*

After the scene in the seclusion of the eastern shore, Jesus now finds himself once more on the populated western shore. Immediately people throng to him again. The *gathering of a crowd* is a consistent detail in the presentation of Mark (3:7ff.; 4:1) but also important for the following story. At first Jairus (" God illumined " or " God awakened," but not a symbolic name) approaches Jesus and, falling at his feet, begs of him to save his daughter (according to verse 42 she is twelve years old). The laying of hands was an old sign of healing. The original purpose was to allow the vivifying strength to flow out into the sick person. For this purpose, one preferred to call elders or pious persons to the sick bed (cf. Jas. 5:14). Because the girl is already dying (according to Matthew and Luke she had already died) great haste is necessary.

For the thought of the evangelist, the father's form of expression is worth considering: *so that she may be made well and live.* The Greek for " make well " can be understood to mean bodily healing and eternal salvation. In the answer of Jesus to the woman with the hemorrhage, " Your faith has made you well," the Christian readers certainly also heard echoes of this deeper meaning. This is not originally implied in the petition of the father; the added phrase " and live " shows the anxiety of the father for the bodily life of his child. For the Hebrews life itself means happiness and salvation; the dominion of death touches mankind in sickness, overpowers him with the death of the body, and with the burial leads him into the kingdom of death. As a healer of the sick, Jesus becomes a giver of life, and when he raises a dead girl to life it is an extreme case of life-giving. This is not far removed from John's thought that Jesus shows himself the " giver of life " in an outstanding sense, as giver of eternal, divine life when he calls back to life a mortally ill person (4:46–54) or one who has been ill for a long time (5:1–9) or even one already in the grave (ch. 11). In " healing " and " raising from the dead " there is a symbolic intimation of the gift of eternal life. This thought has not fully matured in Mark but is already present in germ form.

[35]*While he was still speaking, there came from the ruler's house some who said, " Your daughter is dead. Why trouble the Teacher any further?"* [36]*But ignoring what they said, Jesus said to the ruler of the synagogue, " Do not fear, only believe."* [37]*And he allowed no one to follow him except Peter and James and John the brother of James.* [38]*When they came to the house of the ruler of the synagogue, he saw a tumult, and people weeping and wailing loudly.* [39]*And when he had entered, he said to them, " Why do you make a tumult and weep? The child is not dead but sleeping."* [40]*And they laughed at him. But he put them all outside, and took the child's father and mother and those who were with him, and went in where the child was.* [41]*Taking her by the hand he said to her, " Talitha cumi"; which means,*

" Little girl, I say to you, arise." [12]*And immediately the girl got up and walked; for she was twelve years old. And immediately they were overcome with amazement.* [13]*And he strictly charged them that no one should know this, and told them to give her something to eat.*

The news that the daughter of the ruler of the synagogue had died in the meantime introduces the new scene. It had not been the father's intention to call him to a dead girl, and the messengers also wanted to stop him from coming. This feature of the story as well as the noise and lamentation at the house of mourning and the laughter at Jesus' remark that the girl is only sleeping are mentioned to leave no doubt that death had taken place. But *death* does not stop Jesus either. He hears the news and encourages the father: *Do not fear, only believe.* Thus the theme of faith is here also continued: even before the night of death genuine faith does not capitulate.

To understand the scene at the house of mourning it is important to remember that Jesus wants to avoid any kind of sensation and to prevent a mere belief in the miraculous. But he takes a few qualified witnesses, the three disciples who will later on also witness his transfiguration on the mountain (9:2) and his mortal fear in Gethsemani (14:33f.). After the *resurrection* (cf. 9:9) they can report it, and then the raising of the girl will also appear in a new light. Then Jesus will have entered the heavenly world of glory and overcome the power of death, having first experienced its horror. Although these thoughts are not expressed here, they are intimated for the Christian reader through the three disciples whom Jesus took with him at that time.

That Jesus removes the wailing women and flute players (Jewish mourning custom) is not only for the purpose of performing the miracle in quietness and secret. Jesus knows what is about to happen and, therefore, mourning is not in place. His much disputed words: " The child is not dead but sleeping " point in the same direction. The opinion expressed occasionally that the girl was only apparently dead completely misses the point. Jesus is hinting at his intention here: this *death* is only a passing phenomenon like *sleep*. For believing readers, these words are a revelation: death is only sleep, in the light of faith, from which there is an awakening through the power of God. The young church has retained the old turn of phrase " falling asleep," and looks forward to the future resurrection of the dead. The raising of the daughter of Jairus, however, does not mean that she is experiencing the future resurrection in advance; for the time being she is returning to earthly existence. This resurrection is only a sign, just as in John's gospel the resurrection of Lazarus is a sign, but there it is more closely connected with Christ: he is " the resurrection and the life " (Jn. 11:25).

The raising of the girl occurs in a similar manner to the way the other healings of Jesus are described. He takes the girl by the hand; but all notions of magic are excluded since Jesus calls the girl back to life with *his word of command*. The word is transmitted in Aramaic and it is an intelligible word, not a magical formula: " arise." The result is immediate and so distinguishes this raising from the dead from those of Elijah (1 Kings 17:17-24) and of Elisha (2 Kings 4:29-37). The girl can walk about, a sign that her life strength has returned. Jesus' instruction that the girl be given something to eat is meant to convey that the girl—like the woman with the hemorrhage—is entirely well and will remain so. Those present were overcome with great amazement. That belongs again (like the healing through gesture and word) to the formal construction of the miracle story, but it is also intended to underline this climax in Jesus' ministry of mighty deeds.

Jesus urges the witnesses of the event not to tell anyone of it. This precept of silence ranks with the others of which we have already heard (1 : 34, 44; 3 : 12). In the situation of the time it is meaningless, since all are convinced of the death of the girl and are bound to be extremely amazed at her reawakening. The evangelist, however, has something else in mind: Jesus wishes to hide his *secret* from *unbelievers*. Believers, too, are told that they were not ready to understand the secret of the Son of man. After Jesus' own resurrection this report will reveal and confirm the power of Jesus to overcome death. It will also fortify their faith and be a consolation to them, since the Lord says to all in the face of death: " Do not fear, only believe."

Unbelief and Rejection in His Native Town (6 :1–6a)

¹*He went away from there and came to his own country; and his disciples followed him.* ²*And on the sabbath he began to teach in the synagogue; and many who heard him were astonished, saying, " Where did this man get all this? What is the wisdom given to him? What mighty works are wrought by his hands!* ³*Is not this the carpenter, the son of Mary and brother of James and Joses and Judas and Simon, and are not his sisters here with us? " And they took offense at him.* ⁴*And Jesus said to them, "A prophet is not without honor, except in his own country, and among his own kin, and in his own house." * ⁵*And he could do no mighty work there, except that he laid his hands upon a few sick people and healed them.* ⁶ᵃ*And he marveled because of their unbelief.*

The *unbelieving rejection* of Jesus in his native town of Nazareth stands in contrast to the preceding stories which aimed at awakening faith. The simple woman in the crowd had believed and the ruler of the synagogue, Jairus, had come to him with confidence. In his native town of all places Jesus comes up against rank unbelief. Historically this cannot be doubted (regarding the " brothers " of Jesus cf. Jn. 7:3ff.). But the evangelist is also pursuing a theological interest. Jesus' ministry does not appear unambiguous to his contemporaries. The mystery of his person is not disclosed to them even through his great miracles. Many do not go beyond astonishment (cf. 5:20), and the crowd laughs at him while he raises the daughter of Jairus from the dead. The paradox of unbelief gains special prominence, however, among the Nazarenes; they are typical of those who " see and do not perceive, hear and do not understand " (4:12). This is the same experience and lesson which the fourth evangelist expresses at the end of the public life of Jesus: " Although Jesus had done so many signs before them, they did not believe in him " (Jn. 12:37). Thus the other line of thought, which the evangelist has pursued through this entire section, is uncovered here: the fact and the incomprehensibility of unbelief.

It seems that Jesus is appearing in his native town for the first time as teacher. The presentation is vivid and original. Jesus avails of the right—Luke (4:16-21) depicts it in more detail and more graphically—to which every adult male Israelite was entitled, to perform the scriptural reading and add an explanation. His countrymen are, however, astonished that he is able to speak so well and explain the text. Nothing is said here of Jesus' " authority " (1:22), nor of his challenge that " today " the prophecies are fulfilled (Lk. 4:18). The narrator is not concerned with this here. The point is that there is an *unbelieving astonish-*

ment. Indeed, they speak of miracles performed elsewhere but they refuse to believe in Jesus.

The inhabitants of Nazareth know Jesus as the " carpenter " or (according to other texts) the " son of the carpenter." Jesus helped his father at work and learned the trade that way himself. He is known too as " son of Mary " and " brother " of other men belonging to the family. His " sisters " live there too, also members of the tribe in that area. Hence the people cannot come to terms with the thought that Jesus is something special and they take *offense* at him. This is a typical expression for the unwillingness to believe which has also entered the vocabulary of the community (4 : 17). For all those who read it, it is a serious warning signal : those who think they know Jesus do not understand him and turn their backs on him. There are many impediments and pitfalls for the faith. Even the closest disciples fell away in the dark hour when Jesus allowed his opponents to take him away without resisting (14 : 27, 29).

Jesus reproaches his countrymen with an expression which is probably proverbial : " A prophet is not without honor except in his own country." This expression is also transmitted by John (4 : 44) in a different context and articulates a bitter experience. Those sent by God find contradiction and rejection precisely in their *own country.* Thus Jeremiah is compelled to complain that his countrymen are forging wicked schemes against him and seek to take his life (Jer. 11 : 18–23). It fares no differently with the last One sent by God who transcends all prophets. In the behavior of the Nazarenes Christian readers will find an intimation of the mystery of Jesus' passion. But in the fate of their Lord they also recognize their own calling. Jesus has left his relatives and formed a new " family " (cf. 3 : 35); his disciples have also left everything for the sake of the gospel (10 : 30). The disciple of Christ must be prepared for conflicts in the family for the sake of the faith (cf. 13:12). In the quotation of the prophet, who originally only mentioned " his own country," the evangelist expressly adds that the prophet has no honor either " among his own kin and in his own house." God often does not spare those called by him from this bitterness.

A result of this unbelief is that Jesus cannot perform any great miracle in Nazareth but heals only a few sick by laying his hands on them. Why " could " Jesus not do any mighty work there? Was he limited in his power to perform miracles or inhibited by the unbelief because he needed belief to show his power? Nothing is said about this, neither is there anything of the apologetic information that he *could* not because he *would* not. According to the biblical way of thinking, it is God who grants the power to perform miracles. Hence one must conclude that God has set ends and limits even to the miracle working of Jesus. Jesus *ought* not to perform mighty works where the people shut their minds to him in hard unbelief. His whole ministry stands under the aspect of salvation history, under the *commission of his Father*. It sounds like a commentary when Jesus says in John's gospel: " The Son can do nothing of his own accord, but only what he sees the Father doing " (5:19). Jesus has always refused to do miracles for show, as unbelieving people have demanded of him. He sighs at the wicked generation who demand a sign from heaven (8:11f.). This is also a wholesome lesson for faith, which must not demand visible signs and ultimate proofs. " Jesus marveled at their unbelief "—the account concludes with this sentence and lets the reader reflect further on the riddle of unbelief.

THE MISSION OF THE TWELVE, ATTEMPTS
TO WITHDRAW AND WANDERINGS,
GROWING MISUNDERSTANDING
(6:6b—8:30)

This section forms a new disciple pericope, after the call and election of the twelve. It is the least transparent section in its structure. If we again take note of the historical background, the preaching of the community, and the redaction of the evangelist, the intentions of the evangelist who wanted to compile the traditional material and fashion it into shape will become easier to understand. Viewed historically, after the time of the great Galilean ministry Jesus seems to begin a "restless wandering" which takes him deep into pagan territory (Tyrus, 7:24), and to withdraw into the narrower circle of his disciples. Perhaps, Mark wishes also to give his pagan-Christian readers a hint of Jesus' universality, although his mission remained confined to Israel (cf. 7:27). By way of exception Jesus made use of his healing powers even among the pagans (7:24-30).

Yet even this does not fully cover the purpose which the evangelist has at heart for his readers. In the middle of this moving presentation there is a lengthy instructive passage about "clean and unclean" (7:1-23) which aims at the moral behavior and the life of the community. In this light too one must see the miracle of the loaves (6:30-43), which is meant to have an immediate appeal to the community. It imparts a profound self-understanding to the eucharistic celebrations of the Christian community: the community is the new people of God which God has chosen in his mercy and which Christ the Messianic shepherd gathers about him, making it happy with his presence and serving it with his gifts. Who this giver of divine blessings is is revealed to the disciples in the adjoining theophany story, the walk on the water, even though at that time they did not yet grasp and understand it. Thus historical, catechetical, and redactional aims are mixed and intermingled. The themes comprise again Christ and his community, refer to belief and unbelief, decision and trial, the missionary, ritual, and moral life of the community.

Besides the disciples, who stand out more in this section than they have so far, the people play a not insignificant role. Jesus wants to withdraw from the people because he does not find the right kind of faith in them; but the people continue to go after him and Jesus has pity on them (6:30–34). He feeds them with the word of doctrine and fills them with the bread that he gives. A large crowd has collected in a lonely place in the " wilderness," just as in the past the old Israel collected in the time of grace of the exodus (6:35–43). Also on the western shore the people rush to him again and he heals them (6:53–56). In this way Jesus gathers a new people of God in which the community is meant to recognize itself. But his opponents also make an appearance. Their enmity grows and gives a presentiment of the ignominious end to Jesus' earthly ministry which is also foreshadowed in the end of John the Baptist (6:17–29). For the later community the opponents of Jesus represent a doctrine (7:1–23), an attitude of mind (8:15–18), from which believers in Christ must disassociate themselves and guard against.

Two parallel traditions confronted the evangelist in putting together this account. The reader finds in a sort of duplicated account of each case a miracle of loaves (6:34–43; 8:1–9), a crossing over of the disciples (6:45–52; 8:10), Jesus disputing with his opponents (7:1–23; 8:11f.), a discussion about "bread" (7:24–30; 8:14–21), and a miracle of healing (the deaf man 7:31–37; the blind man at Bethsaida, 8:22–26). These traditional materials are prepared as a continuous narrative, but the summary account and the walking on the water are overdue, and the themes of the discussions are varied in content and of very uneven proportion. The long passage about "clean and unclean" stands in a place of importance about half way in the section. Thus the evangelist will have had roughly the following divisions in mind:

1. The mission of the twelve and their return, the miracle of the loaves and the walking on the water, further activity among the people (6:6b–56);
2. disassociation from a false, precept piety (7:1–23);
3. journeys into pagan territory, growing misunderstanding, the balance of the Galilean ministry (7:24—8:30).

The Mission of the Disciples and Their Return, the Miracle of the Loaves and the Walk on the Water, Further Activity among the People (6:6b–56)

In spite of the unbelief revealed in Jesus' native town, he sends the twelve out in pairs to carry his message into all parts of Galilee. Jesus will not be deterred in his mission and gives the disciples a commission and the authority to work everywhere in his name. The first historical mission of the twelve becomes the prototype of all missions enjoined on the church. To the church, constituted after Easter, devolves the task of taking on the work of Jesus and further realizing it in the world.

The Mission of the Twelve and Missionary Instructions (6 :6b–13)

⁶ᵇ*And he went about the villages teaching.* ⁷*And he called to him the twelve, and began to send them out two by two, and gave them authority over the unclean spirits.* ⁸*He charged them to take nothing for their journey except a staff; no bread, no bag, no money in their belts;* ⁹*but to wear sandals and not put on two tunics.* ¹⁰*And he said to them, " Where you enter a house, stay there until you leave the place.* ¹¹*And if any place will not receive you and they refuse to hear you, when you leave, shake off the dust that is on your feet for a testimony against them."* ¹²*So they went out and preached that men should repent.* ¹³*And they cast out many demons, and anointed with oil many that were sick and healed them.*

This is an ancient report which has retained the local color of Palestine. The introductory remark only serves the purpose of creating a framework: Jesus is in the midst of his Galilean teaching activity but he reaches only a limited circle of small localities and would like to extend his work. For this purpose he makes use of the Twelve whom he had elected earlier (3 : 13–16), and sends them out in pairs. Sending out in pairs is a practice which was also customary in Judaism. In this way not only is the task of the disciples made easier, but they also become *witnesses* concurring in the presentation of God's message. In case of rejection, they will become witnesses in God's court of justice against all who shut their minds to their message (v. 11).

This is not merely a " trial mission " or an insignificant

episode. The disciples are now exercising the function for which
Jesus elected them (3:14f.). Having long enough experienced a
fellowship with Jesus, they are now to share also in Jesus' task
and authority. The twelve *representatives of Israel* elected by
Jesus are obliged to call the Israel of their time to conversion,
giving it signs of the eschatological salvation (casting out demons
and healing) and in case of rejection to become messengers of
judgment. For the evangelist and his readers, this mission of the
disciples becomes a prototype of the mission which is imposed on,
and entrusted to the church. Mission is a salvation happening,
an extension of Jesus' ministry which puts the onus of decision
on the people. It is an offer of salvation in God's name which
leads to judgment only through hardness of heart. The first
mission of the disciples of Jesus is also an admonition and a
mirror of conscience for the later proclaimers of the gospel. The
instructions which Jesus gave to the Twelve in those days retain
their meaning and value for all future messengers of the faith
and urge them to self-criticism as to whether they are fulfilling
their task in the spirit of Jesus.

Jesus permitted the disciples to take a staff for their journey
which was almost indispensable as a protection, and sandals
without which one could not manage on the stony ground of
Palestine. Luke, less acquainted with Palestinian conditions,
forbids even this equipment (Lk. 9:3; 10:4). For Jesus, what is
important is the *spirit of simplicity and frugality*. The disciples
are obliged to renounce all that is unnecessary: provisions and
bag, two tunics and money. They are obliged to seek lodging in
the places to which they come and must not change their quarters
so as not to be entertained and overindulged in other houses.
Their main endeavor must be directed towards the proclamation
of the gospel and the ministry of salvation. The renunciation of

everything superfluous should give emphasis to their message: God's salvation comes to the poor and the sick but it also demands faith and conversion. He who does not receive the messengers of God excludes himself from salvation, faces the judgment of God, and is convicted by his witnesses. As a sign that the messengers have nothing in common with such places they are to shake even the dust off their feet. In spite of external poverty, those sent by Christ are clothed with dignity and power.

The young church understood that the instructions of Jesus which were suited to that time do not remain literally obligatory, as is shown by the divergencies in Matthew and Luke. What counts is the spirit of apostolic simplicity. The words of Jesus, spoken at a moment in history in concrete circumstances, need to be interpreted and applied to changed circumstances. Jesus' challenge to the proclaimers of the gospel, however, must remain undiluted; no mention is made of living a life suitable to one's station. On the other hand, nothing inhuman is required; the young church has also preserved these words of Jesus: " The laborer is worthy of his hire " (Mt. 10:10; Lk. 10:7; cf. 1 Cor. 9:14). The *communities* are obliged to provide their proclaimers of the gospel with the necessities of life.

A single sentence describes the performance of Jesus' charge, the work done by those whom he sent. They " preached " nothing different from Jesus: that the *kingdom of God is at hand*. As to the content, only the exhortation to repentance is mentioned since this is decisive for a sharing in God's kingdom (1:15). The proclamation of the gospel is, as in Jesus' case, bound up with signs of the breakthrough of God's kingdom (1:27, 39; 6:2). The disciples " cast out many demons," in which the kingdom of Satan manifested itself (cf. 3:23–27), and they healed many that were sick, a sign that the time of salvation is at hand. The anointing with oil is only a visible expression of the healing of the sick similar to the laying of hands of Jesus (6:5). It was regarded as an external means by the Jews, and in the case of the disciples it was intended to draw attention to the healing worked by God.

Did the disciples enjoy a great *success* with this mission? We could get this impression, but we hear nothing of the impact the work of the disciples had or of the number of "repentant" people. The course of the gospel presentation leads one to think rather of a failure, or, in any case, not of a rich harvest of faith as Jesus would have wished it. The opinions of the people do not correspond with Jesus' expectations (6:14f.; 8:28), and he himself withdraws more and more from the people. But Mark also had the mission of the young church in mind when he wrote the last sentences in order to articulate the power of the gospel and to encourage the missionaries. If we combine the historical failure with the confirming challenge, then we can believe in the power of God's kingdom without cherishing hopes of success in this world. The word of salvation is effective and the power of God unbroken if we fulfill our duty obediently and faithfully.

Herod Antipas and Jesus (6:14–16)

[14]King Herod heard of it; for Jesus' name had become known. Some said, " John the baptizer has been raised from the dead; that is why these powers are at work in him." [15]But others said, " It is Elijah." And others said, " It is a prophet, like one of the prophets of old." [16]But when Herod heard of it, he said, " John, whom I beheaded, has been raised."

Jesus' sovereign ruler, Herod Antipas, hears of the movement which Jesus has enkindled and begins to take notice. When he received this information cannot be inferred from the gospel passage. In this passage the evangelist wants to intimate the growing *threat to Jesus*. Just as Jesus' Jewish opponents spy on him with suspicion and attack him underhandedly (3:22), so danger threatens him also from political authority. As the proclamation of the gospel is spread over a wider area and gains in power, the counterforces are also rallying.

Herod hears of the *comments of the people*. These public opinions are also important for the evangelist because they disclose the lack of faith in the mass of people as a whole. Although they betray a certain recognition, they do not amount to a belief in the uniqueness of Jesus, his closeness to God, and his Sonship and they show, moreover, an uncertainty of judgment by their diversity. In the first place, there is the opinion that John the Baptist has been raised from the dead, and therefore—as one raised—he now works with greater might through miraculous works (which John never accomplished in his lifetime). It is a Jewish belief that the innocent victim of murder can return, and one tries to " explain " Jesus' astounding activity in this way. In reality it is a flight into vagueness, an evasion of the pressing question, " Who then is this?" (4:41).

It is no different with the second answer, " It is Elijah." They hardly think seriously that one of the great prophets of old has been raised up (cf. Lk. 9:8) but, rather, that God, as in earlier times of need, has raised up an intercessor and helper for them. He who does not find a full faith in Jesus, who classifies him in whatever human categories, fails to meet the kind of response which God expects from mankind with the appearance of his only and beloved Son (cf. 1:11). Every humanly tailored

" explanation " of Jesus is inadequate, worse still, it is unbelief.

" King " Herod subscribes to the first opinion. From the mouth of a hellenist who surely did not believe in a resurrection this is hardly meant seriously. Although he " heard gladly " (6:20) the vigorous preacher of penance, nevertheless, he did not suffer himself to be *converted*. These words are probably meant ironically: " This John, whom I beheaded, has been raised! " With mockery one can endure many a situation (cf. Lk. 23:11). People striving for political power classify everything under their political concepts. Just as Herod unscrupulously had that " just and holy man " imprisoned and executed, so he would also make short work with the " raised John," if he should become a danger to him. This threat hangs over this intermediary account which interrupts the report on the mission of the disciples.

The Death of John the Baptist (6 :17–29)

[17]*For Herod had sent and seized John, and bound him in prison for the sake of Herodias, his brother Philip's wife; because he had married her.* [18]*For John said to Herod, " It is not lawful for you to have your brother's wife."* [19]*And Herodias had a grudge against him, and wanted to kill him. But she could not,* [20]*for Herod feared John, knowing that he was a righteous and holy man, and kept him safe. When he heard him, he was much perplexed; and yet he heard him gladly.* [21]*But an opportunity came when Herod on his birthday gave a banquet for his courtiers and officers and the leading men of Galilee.* [22]*For when Herodias' daughter came in and danced, she pleased Herod and his guests; and the king said to the girl, "Ask me for whatever you wish, and I will grant it."* [23]*And he vowed to her, " Whatever you ask*

me I will give you, even half of my kingdom." ²⁴And she went out, and said to her mother, "What shall I ask?" And she said, "The head of John the baptizer." ²⁵And she came in immediately with haste to the king, and asked, saying, "I want you to give me at once the head of John the Baptist on a platter." ²⁶And the king was exceedingly sorry; but because of his oaths and his guests he did not want to break his word with her. ²⁷And immediately the king sent a soldier of the guard and gave orders to bring his head. He went and beheaded him in prison, ²⁸and brought his head on a platter, and gave it to the girl; and the girl gave it to her mother. ²⁹When his disciples heard of it, they came and took his body and laid it in a tomb.

This appended story spans the time the disciples are on their first mission. It tells of the death of the great preacher of penance from the Jordan, the precursor of Jesus who, in the evangelist's view, appears in the role of Elijah and of whom it is later written: " and they did to him whatever they pleased " (9:13). The similarities with the fate of the old prophet whom the pagan Queen Jezebel, the consort of King Achab, pursued with deadly hate (1 Kings 19:2) are unmistakable. In contrast with Elijah, however, John falls victim to the malice of Herodias and suffers a gruesome death. The *might of evil* triumphs over the " righteous and holy man," an omen for the Messiah, who will go the same road.

Mark adopts a popular version of the death of John the Baptist. He is not troubled about the historical details. Herodias was not the wife of Philip before Herod Antipas married her; she was the wife of another stepbrother of the Galilean ruler also called Herod (" without land "). Philip was another stepbrother and also a Tetrarch (Lk. 3:1) who later married the daughter of

Herodias. The Jewish historian Flavius Josephus alleges political motives for the execution. The evangelist is concerned with the shocking circumstances which this popular narrative has, not implausibly, recorded. The daughter of Herodias (according to Flavius Josephus, called Salome) aroused with her dance, which was unusual for a princess, the favor of the guests and the sovereign. Herod wants to show himself a king—not unusual—and promises her a gift. " Even half of my kingdom " is a boastful turn of phrase reminiscent of the words of the Great King of Persia spoken to Queen Esther also at a wine feast (Est. 7:2). Herod strengthens his words by an oath which later causes embarrassment. The oath, to be sure, was not binding in view of the horrible request; but such considerations are ignored. The king wants to " keep face " and not break his word in front of the guests. So he gives the fatal command, a weak and criminal compliance which easily reminds the Christian reader of *Pilate's behavior* at the trial of Jesus.

In consequence of frivolous, worldly conduct, against which his call to penance warned, through the malice of a woman and the weakness of a king, the man of God found his *death*. The power of darkness is revealed in the senselessness, indeed, the absurdity of what took place in those days in the fortress of Machaerus. For even according to pagan sensibilities, the birthday of a king should be marked by deeds of mercy, by the release of prisoners. Here the exact opposite takes place: the high-spirited celebration leads to a macabre scene during the banquet, a ghastly event even for ancient peoples. It is the same darkness which lies, even more oppressively, over the hour " the Son of man is betrayed into the hand of sinners " (14:41). Thus in the midst of the outwardly hopeful ministry of Jesus in Galilee there appears a dark omen of the terrible end which God in his incomprehensible counsel has decided for his Messiah.

Perhaps the final remark that the disciples of John came and buried his body is not without significance. It is, as it were, a consoling conclusion: the man of God has found peace. And it articulates a cheering prospect: the Crucified is also laid in a *tomb* over which the message of the resurrection resounds.

The Return of the Disciples and the Vain Attempt to Withdraw from the People (6 :30-34)

[30]*The apostles returned to Jesus, and told him all that they had done and taught.* [31]*And he said to them, " Come away by yourselves to a lonely place, and rest a while." For many were coming and going and they had no leisure even to eat.* [32]*And they went away in the boat to a lonely place by themselves.* [33]*Now many saw them going, and knew them, and they ran there on foot from all the towns, and got there ahead of them.* [34]*As he landed he saw a great throng, and he had compassion on them, because they were like sheep without a shepherd; and he began to teach them many things.*

The return of the disciples gives the impression that their mission had been successful. This seems to explain the great thronging of people. It is, however, noticeable that they only report in general terms " all that they had done and taught." The whole item is meant to reflect the future picture of Christian missions. The disciples are " apostles " here, perhaps, in the original sense of " those sent forth;" but the later permanent designation " apostle " for Christian missionaries is already evoked. Now we also hear that they *taught*. They exercise the same activity so often ascribed to Jesus and which remains of significance for the later community. In the ministry of Jesus and of his first disciples there occurs as source and parable what the young church is charged with.

Thus the request of Jesus to go to a lonely place and rest for a while will also have a significance transcending the situation. Indeed it fits outwardly well into the framework and is underlined by the reason given which follows. Viewed historically, however, the escape of Jesus to the quiet eastern shore is not quite transparent. According to Matthew, Jesus withdraws intentionally because he had heard of Herod's actions. Luke only speaks generally of Jesus' withdrawal to the territory of Bethsaida, and he later records a statement according to which Jesus will definitely not allow Herod to influence him into relinquishing his task (13:31–33). Mark mentions still further withdrawal attempts of Jesus (6:45; 7:24; 8:10). So yet another tendency is implied here: Jesus wants to get away from the Galilean people because they cannot produce the faith he expects of them. He gradually withdraws into the *circle of disciples*. The latter becomes the image of the *later community,* in which, besides missionary work, there is room for inner recollection and reflection. Two things, outward activity and inward retreat, belong to the Christian life (cf. Lk. 10:38–42).

But the people will not leave Jesus alone. They take note of his departure and follow him into solitude. Again Jesus finds himself surrounded by a great crowd and he has compassion on them because they are *like sheep without a shepherd*. When he gathers them around him and teaches them once again, it is not merely human compassion. The image of the scattered sheep without a shepherd is taken from the Old Testament.

The Great Meal (6 :35–44)

[35]*And when it grew late, his disciples came to him and said,
" This is a lonely place, and the hour is now late;* [36]*send them
away, to go into the country and villages round about and buy
themselves something to eat."* [37]*But he answered them, " You
give them something to eat." And they said to him, " Shall we
go and buy two hundred denarii worth of bread, and give it to
them to eat? "* [38]*And he said to them, " How many loaves have
you? Go and see." And when they had found out, they said,
" Five, and two fish."* [39]*Then he commanded them all to sit
down by companies upon the green grass.* [40]*So they sat down in
groups, by hundreds and by fifties.* [41]*And taking the five loaves
and two fish he looked up to heaven, and blessed, and broke the
loaves, and he gave them to the disciples to set before the people;
and he divided the two fish among them all.* [42]*And they all ate
and were satisfied.* [43]*And they took up twelve baskets full of
broken pieces and of fish.* [44]*And those who ate the loaves were
five thousand men.*

The great meal in a lonely place, related here in simple language,
represents a climax in the ministry of Jesus among the people
which has also a deeper symbolic significance. The *time of grace
of the journey through the wilderness,* which in Judaism was
regarded as a prototype of the Messianic time, is repeated. The
" desert milieu " of that time is clearly recorded. Not only the
" lonely place " reminds one of it, but also the seating in the
open and the division into groups of a hundred and of fifty (cf.
Ex. 18:25). Jesus appears as a second Moses (more clearly in
Jn. 6:14, 32), collecting the people of God (cf. v. 34), and gives
them in the wilderness the life-preserving bread from God. In

this salvation-theological sense Jesus is the Messiah, the promised Messianic prophet according to the prophecy of Moses (cf. Jn. 6:14). The Christian community is to become conscious of itself as the new community of God in which the old promises are fulfilled.

The content of this portrayal is, however, still richer in meaning for the Christian readers. From this action of Jesus they look ahead to that holy meal which Jesus instituted at the *last supper*. At the eucharistic celebration they join their master in an intimate banquet which will find its final consummation in the kingdom of God (cf. 14:25). The " green grass " which can be found in that region only in spring suggests the time of the Passover (cf. Jn. 6:4), with which the last supper is also connected. This connection is not emphasized by Mark; he does not say that Jesus intentionally stays away from the Passover in Jerusalem and that he intends to celebrate a different, a new Passover with the people of God. But such thoughts are apt and received further attention in the young church (cf. Jn. 6:4).

Our Mark account is the oldest of the meal narratives of the four evangelists. It preserves the style of a Marcan presentation, especially in its *focus on Jesus,* who acts quietly and purposefully avoiding all sensationalism. After the great miracle, Jesus urges the disciples to depart immediately. He dismisses the crowd and withdraws into the hills to pray (vv. 45f.). The reaction of the participants is not portrayed. The disciples, at that time, did not grasp the full significance of the event either (cf. v. 52). Jesus' conversation with them before the multiplication of bread shows that their thoughts are imprisoned in superficialities. Their Master's request that they should feed the crowd embarrasses them. Their purse contains 200 denarii with which they would be willing to buy bread. But Jesus asks them about their own provisions, and they ascertain that five loaves and two fish are there. As they act under Jesus' direction, the miracle is wrought through their hands. After the people have sat down in not too large groups, the disciples share out the bread and fish and afterwards they collect the remains, twelve baskets full. The deeper thoughts contained in this marvelous event were not revealed to them until later, when they recognized the true nature of Jesus. The believing readers, however, could and should already glean a deeper significance from this portrayal.

But Jesus' actions are the center of interest here. He takes the five loaves and two fish and looks up to heaven. That is a special gesture which suggests Jesus' confidence in his heavenly *Father* and his inner harmony with him; at their grace before meals the Jews usually looked down at the bread in their hands. But what Jesus does then is no different from what the father of a family used to do at table: he says grace and breaks the flat slices of bread into pieces and shares them out to those present. But this taking and blessing, this breaking and giving reminds one of what he did at the last supper (14:22). In that lonely place Jesus divides the bread among the hungry crowd and all are satisfied. In spite of the needy, wretched circumstances it is a holy and marvelous meal, a Messianic meal with God's people.

At the last supper, only a small number of disciples are gathered in the room about him; but they represent the future community, and the farewell meal gains a unique significance through the new and holy institution of Jesus. This eating of bread and drinking of wine gives one a share in the body and blood of God's servant who gives himself up to die for the many. From this bread the new people of God live, a people gathered from many nations. Thus the scene in the wilderness, as many people of the old Israel are gathered about Jesus, remains significant. It becomes an image of the Christian community in the world. The faithful have found in Jesus their shepherd and leader. He prepares for them the *table of the word and of bread*, he teaches and nourishes them. Through him they have become a holy community living in the world yet detached from it. They are still a pilgrim people of God but they live under the blessing of the Messianic era.

Jesus Walks on the Water (6 :45–52)

[45]Immediately he made his disciples get into the boat and go before him to the other side, to Bethsaida, while he dismissed the crowd. [46]And after he had taken leave of them, he went into the hills to pray. [47]And when evening came, the boat was out on the sea, and he was alone on the land. [48]And he saw that they were distressed in rowing, for the wind was against them. And about the fourth watch of the night he came up to them, walking on the sea. He meant to pass by them, [49]but when they saw him walking on the sea, they thought it was a ghost, and cried out; [50]for they all saw him, and were terrified. But immediately he spoke to them and said, " Take heart, it is I; have no fear." [51]And he got into the boat with them and the wind ceased. And they were utterly astounded, [52]for they did not understand about the loaves, but their hearts were hardened.

The story of Jesus' walk on the water, which is linked with the miracle of the loaves also by Matthew and John (in Luke everything down to the confession of Peter is missing), records an experience of the disciples which has made a deep impression on these intimate companions of Jesus. The individual presentations diverge not inconsiderably from one another in some tones (John) and peculiarities (Matthew); but they all reach their peak in the encounter of Jesus with the disciples on the sea and the sublime and consoling words of Jesus: " Take heart, it is I; have no fear." After the Messianic revelation of Jesus before the people at the great meal, he now reveals himself to his disciples immediately in his superhuman greatness, in an epiphany which discloses the *mystery of his divine essence*. Matthew has made this clear for his readers by having the disciples in the ship fall down before Jesus to confess: " Truly you are the Son of God " (Mt. 14:33). But Mark leaves a veil over this unique experience, and through the disciples' lack of understanding he lets it be known that the meaning of the event did not, and could not, dawn on them at that time because they were not meant to understand it until after the resurrection of Jesus. Any brooding over the historical event is just as futile as pondering over the apparitions of the risen Lord. Only he who believes in the resurrection of Christ can accept the fact of this numinous happening, this epiphany of the divine in the earthly sphere, and understand the meaning of the apparitions of Jesus. The disciples' lack of understanding that night on the Sea of Galilee is an exhortation for the community to believe in the risen Lord and to view his earthly life in this light.

Within the Marcan presentation, too, there are several discrepancies. The destination to " Bethsaida," a place situated on the northern shore of the sea, is not quite intelligible. The truth is that the disciples land at the plain of Gennesaret in the west. The first record of the time of day, " and when evening came," allows for a long interval between evening and Jesus' walk on the water. " About the fourth watch " which refers to the last hours of the night. Were the disciples all that time on the sea?

With a strong contrary wind blowing that would not be impossible. Why does Jesus mean to pass them by? One would expect him to climb directly into the boat with them. After the encounter the wind ceased. Is that considered to be a miraculous event like the calming of the storm? Nothing is said about this. We are leaving these questions aside and will try to understand the narrative with regard to the narrator's intention.

Mark portrays the whole as an epiphany, as an illumination of Jesus' divine glory before his disciples. The abrupt departure to which Jesus urges his disciples is noteworthy. It says: he *made* them immediately get into the boat. Jesus seems to follow a special plan. Indeed, there is a good reason why he does not go with them: he wants to dismiss the crowd. After the dismissal, Jesus goes into the " hills " to pray. This seeking of the hills which indicated the proximity of God (cf. 9:2) and his remaining in prayer (cf. 1:35) already point to a special plan. Verse 47 depicts the situation in the late hours of the evening: the boat with the disciples is on the sea; Jesus alone is on the land. But not until Jesus sees how laboriously they are rowing, since they have a contrary wind, does he come to them by walking on the waves. In the meantime, nearly all the night has passed. This can hardly be understood otherwise than that Jesus intentionally awaited this hour and situation in order to reveal himself to his disciples. Now the following remark, " He meant to pass by them," makes sense. They were meant to see something of his *glory,* like Moses when God's glory " passed by " him on Mt. Sinai (Ex. 33:21-23), or like Elijah on Horeb when the Lord passed by him in a soft whisper (1 Kings 19:11f.). Jesus " came to them " as Yahweh came to the old men of God, not in the fullness of his majesty but in a mysterious approach which assures them of his presence. The disciples should have drawn consolation and strength from the proximity and grace of their Lord's presence.

Nevertheless, the disciples understand nothing. They think they are seeing a ghost and cry out loud. They could not doubt the apparition itself; "they all saw him," but it terrified them. Then Jesus reveals himself to them in an unmistakable manner. "Immediately he spoke to them"; he does not wish them to think him a ghost. His address to them disperses all fear. They hear the familiar sound of his words. He says to them: "Take heart, it is I; have no fear." With the words *it is I* he first lets himself be known; but it has another, deeper meaning. It is the sublime "I am" which is characteristic for the self-revelation of the Old Testament God to the people of his covenant. Yahweh promises his servant Israel help and salvation with these words: "that you may know and believe me and understand that I am he . . . I, I am the Lord and besides me there is no saviour" (Is. 43:10f.). It is not only a majestic revelation but one which promises protection and blessing. Hence the words of Jesus are also meant to disperse all anxiety and fear: "have no fear."

The evangelist's final remark connects the multiplication of bread closely with the walk on the water. If the disciples had understood the happening in the wilderness, they would also have been able to interpret the epiphany of Jesus on the nocturnal sea. The *giver of life* is also the *conqueror of death*. In the Old Testament the depths of the water are regarded as an evil power. But God "tramples the waves of the sea" (Job 9:8); his throne is established high above the roaring of the flood (Ps. 93:2ff.); he can rescue from mighty waters (Ps. 144:7). The walk of Jesus on the water is a revelation of divine might; his coming to the disciples a promise of protection and salvation. What he is to the people he wishes in greater measure to be to the disciples: bringer of redemption and saviour. To them too is revealed that his Messiahship transcends all Jewish expectation He is not just the earthly helper of those in need, a second Moses, the prophet of the final time. He is not a human figure at all but filled with divine powers. Still more: he is himself of divine nature, God's true Son.

On the Plain of Gennesaret (6:53–56)

[53]*And when they had crossed over, they came to land at Gennesaret, and moored to the shore. [54]And when they got out of the boat, immediately the people recognized him, [55]and ran about the whole neighborhood and began to bring sick people on their pallets to any place where they heard he was. [56]And wherever he came, in villages, cities, or country, they laid the sick in the market places, and besought him that they might touch even the fringe of his garment; and as many as touched it were made well.*

Mark also concludes this section with a summary account (as 3:7–12). Artistically, he wants to bring to a close the excursion of Jesus to the eastern shore (6:31) which led to the great meal, and so also round off the composition concerning the mission of the disciples and its impact on the people. The summary account, of which he is author, offers nothing new as to content but rather takes up themes which had already been explored. The great thronging of the crowd continues unabated, the sick want to touch him (3:10; 5:28), because a power of healing goes out from him (cf. 5:30). After the great self-revelation of Jesus at the miracle of the loaves and the walk on the water, the evangelist returns to the accustomed picture and demonstrates that the behavior of the people had not changed: they seek him as a popular saviour and worker of miracles; but no deeper faith is germinating in them. After the divine epiphany of Jesus before his disciples, the lonely event on the nocturnal sea, the account takes the reader back again into the Galilean ministry of Jesus among the people. In spite of all the closeness and " touching," one feels the inner *distance* Jesus keeps from the people. Jesus does not withdraw from the people, any more than he withdrew from those who followed him into the lonely place. There he taught them; here he heals them again.

Mark depicts Jesus here as a " divine human being " from whom go out miraculous powers of healing. Such ideas were also current among the pagans of Hellenism. Jesus appears as the helper and physician of the poor and sick people. After the miracle of the loaves and the walk on the water the believing readers know more clearly that he is more than a Hellenistic miracle worker and saviour. His power comes from God himself; it is rooted in the mystery of his unique Sonship of God.

Jesus Disassociates Himself from the False, Precept Piety of the Jews (7:1-23)

The following section, like the other instructive passages in Mark's gospel, has from the outset a stronger theological significance; it sets the Christian reader an immediate challenge. Historically, the Galilean scene is held on to—a few scribes had come from Jerusalem (cf. 3:22)—but the spiritual panorama is wider: those Pharisees and scribes speak as representatives of the Jewish precept religion. The readers have already heard of conflicts regarding the law (the question about the sabbath, 2:23-28 and 3:1-6). Spying on Jesus and suspicion of him are nothing new (cf. 2:1-22). Earlier, Jesus had come to his disciples' defense, but the conflict now takes on the aspect of a matter of principle. What is at stake here is not any particular transgression of the law as expounded by the Pharisees—here the Levitical cult of purification—but rather that the disciples do not observe the "tradition of the elders." Jesus is not afraid of breaking down this "fence" built around the divine law and giving a new significance to the pure will of God. He sharply criticizes the externalized piety of the Judaism of his day. This gives him the opportunity to speak about true "cleanliness" and to demand a morality which issues from the heart and from the mind, thereby highlighting the foundations of Christian morality. That Jesus is here meant to address the community can be inferred from the fact that the disciples once again (as in the case of the parables) receive special instructions apart from the people ("in the house," v. 17).

Precepts of Men and God's Law (7 :1-13)

[1]*Now when the Pharisees gathered together to him, with some of the scribes, who had come from Jerusalem,* [2]*they saw that some of his disciples ate with hands defiled, that is, unwashed.* [3]*(For the Pharisees, and all the Jews, do not eat unless they wash their hands, observing the tradition of the elders;* [4]*and when they come from the market place, they do not eat unless they purify themselves; and there are many other traditions which they observe, the washing of cups and pots and vessels of bronze.)* [5]*And the Pharisees and scribes asked him, "Why do your disciples not live according to the tradition of the elders, but eat with hands*

defiled? " [6]*And he said to them, " Well did Isaiah prophesy of you hypocrites, as it is written, ' This people honors me with their lips, but their heart is far from me;* [7]*in vain do they worship me, teaching as doctrine the precepts of men.'* [8]*You leave the commandments of God and hold fast to the tradition of men."*

The Pharisees (cf. 2:16, 18, 24) were an organized brotherhood or religious party about whom we can easily have a wrong conception. In no way do they have to be " hypocrites," in our sense of the word, who parade a sham piety to the public gaze. They wanted to fulfill all precepts conscientiously in fidelity to the laws of the elders in order to receive God's favor and to obtain a share in the promised salvation of God in the " future eon." They wanted to raise the entire people to a priestly holiness and thus hasten the coming of the Messianic age. Because of their serious endeavor and commitment to the well-being of the people, they enjoyed a high respect in wide segments of the population. To be sure, in their zeal they laid the highest value on the smallest precept of the law.

They were not satisfied with the commandments of the Old Testament but observed, over and above this, many regulations which their scribes had evolved through interpretation and application of the Old Testament law. These are the *traditions of the elders* which Jesus attacks. The precepts for purification of which we read were originally meant for the priests exercising ritualistic service at the sanctuary; but the Pharisees wanted to extend these to the entire people and to everyday life so as to prepare for God a priestly and holy people. The detailed precepts of the " tradition of the elders " were placed at a level with the law of Moses and meant a heavy burden for the people in their daily lives. Jews who did not observe them were called that " crowd who do not know the law " (cf. Jn. 7 : 49) and were despised as transgressors of the law.

The Pharisaical brotherhood was widespread over the entire country; the scribes had their schools for the most part in Jerusalem where they gathered pupils about themselves. Now some of them have come to Galilee and have noticed that the disciples of Jesus do not observe the prescribed washing before meals. It is not simply a matter of a lack of cleanliness but a neglect of the ritual precepts of purification. Mark enlightens his readers a little here: generally one had to purify oneself before meals at least with a " handful " of water. When returning from the market, where there was a greater danger of Levitical defile-ment (through dealing with pagans), one had to immerse one's arm up to the elbow in a large receptacle (cf. Jn. 2:6). Finally, also prescribed was the rinsing of pots and cups and others vessels. Jesus swept aside these petty distinctions, these human regula-tions, with a single citation from the *prophets*. The prophets had often raised their voices against an externalized ritual piety and had demanded an honesty of mind, moral probity, and the exercise of penance. Not service with the lips but the closeness of the heart to God, not human precepts but God's commandment: that is Jesus' challenge to his critics.

The citation from Isaiah probably meant much to the young church. They sought a spiritual, morally fruitful form of worship and desired to offer God " spiritual sacrifices " (1 Pet. 2:5), acts of love made possible by the Holy Spirit. One must not, how-ever, take these words out of their historical context. Not every kind of cult is rejected here, only a service *with the lips* with its corresponding *frame of mind,* a ritualistic narrowness which forgets and neglects the moral-holy will of God for the sake of external regulations.

⁹And he said to them, " You have a fine way of rejecting the commandment of God, in order to keep your tradition! ¹⁰For Moses said, ' Honor your father and your mother '; and, ' He who speaks evil of father or mother, let him surely die '; ¹¹but you say, ' If a man tells his father or his mother, What you would have gained from me is Corban ' (that is, given to God)— ¹²then you no longer permit him to do anything for his father and mother, ¹³thus making void the word of God through your tradition which you hand on. And many such things you do."

Jesus selects an especially rank case to show that human statutes can lead to a neglect of the law of God. The duty to honor father and mother, not to " speak evil of them," and to support old and needy parents was enjoined by *God's commandment* and, of course, was also accepted by the scribes. But the keeping of a vow was also a holy duty. It used to happen that a Jew made a gift to the temple through the " Corban " vow. Then he said: " This is to be a a holy offering (Corban) " and so he withdrew the things involved from profane use, that is, also from his parents' use. Later this became a formula whereby many goods were denied others even without having first handed them to the temple. This injury to one's parents done through a Corban vow must have already occurred in the time of Jesus. Jesus places the commandment of love above burnt offerings and other sacrifices (12:33) and does not permit the neglect of one's duty to one's parents even through a vow. God does not desire honor and love at the cost of *love for one's neighbor.* He who interprets the scriptures in that way sets up human regulations and ignores the will of God. It is an example of Jesus' sovereign decision in questions of law (cf. 1:22), of his unerring advocacy of the things of God (cf. 10:6–9), but also of his knowledge that God is love and desires nothing but love, love of one's neighbor whereby he himself is loved. It is the basic principle which he has set up for all our actions: love of God and one's neighbor are insolubly bound up together (12:30f.). He who loves God must also love his brother. Love overrides all legalism.

Clean and Unclean (7:14-23)

14And he called the people to him again, and he said to them, " Hear me, all of you, and understand: 15there is nothing outside a man which by going into him can defile him; but the things which come out of a man are what defile him." [16a If any man has ears to hear, let him hear."] 17And when he had entered the house, and left the people, his disciples asked him about the parable. 18And he said to them, " Then you are also without understanding? Do you not see that whatever goes into a man from outside cannot defile him, 19since it enters, not his heart but his stomach, and so passes on?" (Thus he declared all foods clean.) 20And he said, " What comes out of a man is what defiles a man. 21For from within, out of the heart of a man, come evil thoughts, fornication, theft, murder, adultery, 22coveting, wickedness, deceit, licentiousness, envy, slander, pride, foolishness. 23All these evil things come from within, and they defile a man."

After a conflict with his opponents, Jesus calls the people together in order to impart an important doctrine to them— a hint for the Christian community to listen to the words of the Master. The occasion, the ritual washing of hands (v. 2), has receded into the background, for Jesus' words to the people do not touch on ablution but food and its consumption. Jesus' teaching in no way refers only to individual Jewish regulations. It deals with the basic question as to what is the meaning of *clean and unclean*. With a parable-type conundrum he urges his listeners to think. The saying is difficult to understand in its general form; but the aim is to have the people " hear and understand," as in the parable instruction (ch. 4). The phrase " If any man . . ." (v. 16) is the same as the one at the end of the parable of the sower (4:9); it is, however, only partially attested and most likely not original. Anything further which Jesus said to the people and how the people reacted to his words is not recorded. The interpretation is reserved for the inner circle of Jesus' disciples, those about him (4:10), and is thereby presented to the believing Christian community.

The meaning of the conundrum had not dawned on the disciples either; but since they are faithful men willing to believe, Jesus discloses everything to them " in the house "—as he did in the case of the parables and later in other places (9:28, 33; 10:10). The disciples' lack of understanding belongs to the earthly activity of Jesus just as much as the " Messiah secret " does, and it is a constant exhortation to meditate with faith more thoroughly on his words and deeds. Jesus explains to the disciples that at the base of the conundrum is the image of food which, entering a man from the outside, goes its natural way. Jesus speaks unconstrainedly of things natural. The consumption and elimination of food is a natural process which has nothing to do with " cleanliness " in a moral and religious sense. That is for the Jews—who held on to the old notions of the " uncleanliness " of certain animals and food, and of defilement through natural processes (sexual intercourse) and through contact (with lepers and corpses), and generally guarded several ritual " taboos "—a liberal and daring point of view.

More important for Jesus is the second part of his pronounce-ment, which deals with real " defilement." From *within man,* out of the heart of man, come thoughts and desires which lead to wicked deeds and vices. Here Jesus has revealed the decisive principle of morality, that the root of morality lies in the decision of man's conscience, and, at the same time, he has taken the religious life into the sphere of morality and spiritualized it. This was a necessary clarification for the time; for us now it has become self-evident. But even today the reference to the tendency of the human heart to give birth to wicked thoughts and desires is not superfluous. Jesus knows the human heart whose " imagi-nation is evil from its youth " (Gen. 8:21), although God has created man according to his image (Gen. 9:6). Despite all affirmation of the creature and his goodness as a creature, despite all high estimation of man and his likeness to God, the experi-ence of this world shows that man has a dark and enigmatic inclination towards evil which is the source of immorality, sin, and vice. It is remarkable that Jesus does not speak here of the pure and good thoughts and deeds of man. This is due in part to the question: " What defiles a man? " But a certain pessi-mism in the moral estimation of man remains unmistakable. This is connected with Jesus' demand for repentance which is addressed to all listeners without exception. Paul has interpreted Jesus' teaching correctly: " all have sinned and fall short of the glory of God " (Rom. 3:23).

So we are not surprised that a long catalogue of vices follows. At the beginning of the catalogue of vices stand wicked deeds which today as in the past belong to the most frequent sins and crimes committed: fornication, theft, murder. Next, three simi-lar vices are named: adultery, coveting, wickedness. In the third group, envy (" the evil eye ") is noteworthy; in the Old Testament it meant both sexual lust and envious, possessive looks. In the last group, " slander " probably refers to abusive talk against one's fellows, suitably paired with " pride " or " arrogance," that spiritual sin which shuts a man off from his fellows and from God. Hence, the last item, " foolishness," probably has a deeper meaning than it usually has with us. In the Bible, the " foolish man " is the man who " does not know God," who forgets God in his blindness and self-sufficiency, and despises him (cf. Ps. 10:3f.; 14:1; Lk. 12:20).

Mark, who does not transmit Jesus' sermon on the mount, has preserved for us here a nucleus of Jesus' moral teaching. He shows us Jesus in his whole moral seriousness but also in his deep knowledge of the human heart. This lesson is an invaluable sign-post towards recognizing that the *inside* of man, his conscience or, as Jesus puts it, his *heart* is the source and decisive factor in good and evil behavior. When the heart of man is pure and clear then from it will come, as from a clear spring, good thoughts and deeds.

Journeys into Pagan Territory, Growing Misunderstanding, the Balance of the Galilean Ministry (7:24—8:30)

After the conflict with Jewish legalism, it seems to be the intention of the evangelist to direct his reader's attention towards the pagan world. To be sure, only one single story from tradition is at his disposal: the healing of the possessed daughter of the pagan woman of Syrophoenicia (7:24-30). He has put this story unheralded at the beginning of this section. For Jesus and his disciples there begins a time of " movement from place to place "; but from the place names given and the travel notes (7:31; 8:10, 13, 22, 27) one cannot form a clear picture of Jesus' itinerary. Excluding 7:31, the evangelist does not attempt to link the individual stories together. Above all, the report on the second meal is introduced only with the remarks, " in those days " (8:1); so it seems doubtful whether Mark is thinking of pagan territory and pagans as partakers of the meal. Jesus returns from the north in a curved route to the Sea of Galilee (7:31); there the healing of the deaf mute occurs. After the (second) miracle of loaves, Jesus once more crosses the sea (8:10). Then Jesus arrives again at Bethsaida, at the northern end of the sea, and heals the blind man (8:22-26). From there in a northerly direction one can reach Caesarea Philippi, again pagan territory, where the interrogation of the disciples and Peter's confession took place (8:27-30); but that Jesus went there directly from Bethsaida with his disciples is not recorded.

The Pagan Woman of Syrophoenicia (7 24-30)

[24]*And from there he arose and went to the region of Tyre and Sidon. And he entered a house, and would not have anyone know it; yet he could not be hid.* [25]*But immediately a woman, whose little daughter was possessed by an unclean spirit, heard of him, and came and fell down at his feet.* [26]*Now the woman was a Greek, a Syrophoenician by birth. And she begged him to cast the demon out of her daughter.* [27]*And he said to her, " Let the children first be fed, for it is not right to take the children's bread and throw it to the dogs."* [28]*But she answered him, " Yes, Lord; yet even the dogs under the table eat the children's crumbs."* [29]*And he said to her, " For this saying you*

may go your way; the demon has left your daughter." [30]And she went home, and found the child lying in bed, and the demon gone.

In this story, a pearl of tradition, a pagan woman, Syrophoenician (of the southern part of the long coastal strip) by birth, demonstrates that she possesses a faith which is similar to and as strong as that of the hemorrhaging woman, neither is she put out by the initial refusal of Jesus. The metaphorical words of Jesus convey that *he has first and foremost been sent to the children of Israel and must not show preference to the pagans.* It has often been pointed out that the Jews considered themselves to be children of God and at times with contempt called the pagans " dogs," which in the Orient is strongly abusive. But this refers to the wild street dogs. Jesus speaks of the " little dogs," by which he means domestic animals, and that is how the woman understands him. Hence Jesus is not using abusive language but, as he often does, he is creating a metaphor to illustrate an idea. The addition of " first " is often found to be noteworthy. Did Mark himself add this word with respect to Christian mission? Is it not his own aim here, while acknowledging Israel's priority in salvation history, to open a door for pagans (cf. Rom. 1:16; 2:9f.)? However, the word belongs inseparably to the sentence as it stands, and the substantiation which follows does not aim at making the food of the little dogs a point at issue; it only underlines the priority which the children have. The words of Jesus do not convey a total refusal but are only an indication of his obligation to bring the blessings of the time of salvation first and foremost to Israel. This also corresponds to his customary attitude; for although he confined his mission to the Jewish people, he did not thereby exclude the pagans from salvation. He expected that they would come from east and west to share in the kingdom of God (Mt. 8:11). Mark had given a hint of this "coming" of the pagans into the kingdom in the portrayal 3:8, and he also sees the Syrophoenician woman in this light.

The woman takes up the image used by Jesus and turns it with ready wit to her own advantage: even the little dogs under the table eat the crumbs from the children's bread. "For this saying" Jesus grants her request and utters the word of healing even at a distance. Does Jesus allow himself to be overcome by the riposte of the woman? No, he merely rewards the woman's strong *confidence* in him, which was of a clever simplicity. She seized the opportunity as the hemorrhaging woman did. Jesus does not need to change his conviction and intention: the woman had only apparently "changed his mind." In reality the principle which he enunciated allowed for this exception and he could only hope that the faith of the woman was strong enough to recognize this possibility and to seize it. It is idle to ask whether Jesus wished to test her faith. The fact remains that it was a test for her and she passed it brilliantly.

The Healing of Deaf Mute (7:31–37)

[31]*Then he returned from the region of Tyre, and went through Sidon to the Sea of Galilee, through the region of the Decapolis.* [32]*And they brought to him a man who was deaf and had an impediment in his speech; and they besought him to lay his hands upon him.* [33]*And taking him aside from the multitude privately, he put his fingers into his ears, and he spat and touched his tongue;* [34]*and looking up to heaven he sighed, and*

said to him, Ephphatha," that is, " Be opened." [35]*And his ears were opened, his tongue was released, and he spoke plainly.* [36]*And he charged them to tell no one; but the more he charged them, the more zealously they proclaimed it.* [37]*And they were astonished beyond measure, saying, " He has done all things well; he even makes the deaf hear and the dumb speak."*

The people bring a deaf man to Jesus who because of his hearing defect can only speak with difficulty, perhaps, stammer or stutter: a picture of human misery. They beg Jesus, after their manner of thinking, that he may lay hands on him and so give him relief or healing. This human need touches Jesus' heart. He puts his finger into the ears of the deaf man and touches his tongue with spittle. In that way he accommodates himself to the people's mentality and leaves no doubt that he intends to heal the evil. But that is only the preparation; the healing itself follows after a word of command. Jesus speaks it on his own authority, but after he has looked up to heaven and gained his heavenly Father's approval. As the sigh indicates, he is himself very moved. The Aramaic word preserved and translated for the readers is not directed to the sick organs but to the patient himself: " Be opened." From the Jewish point of view, the whole man is sick, and when he gets well this has its effect on the sick organs. The result is immediate: the ears are opened and the tongue is released (a metaphor for the speech impediment). Although this report is antiquated and many elements sound strange to us (e.g., the medicinal value of spittle), the portrayal, nevertheless, remains a striking illustration of what happens when Jesus heals: the *whole man* is healed. The infirmities which distort God's creation are removed, the original brilliance of creation becomes once more visible. It is a sign of the new creation which God will inaugurate at some time in the future. In the morning of creation he has " done all things well " (Gen. 1); on the day of consummation he will " make all things new " (Rev. 21:5).

According to the ancient account the healing took place *aside from the multitude*. The evangelist who is so much concerned with the secrecy and the preservation of the secrecy of Jesus' miracles has hardly invented this trait. At the most, he strengthened it (" privately "). In the related story of the blind man, Jesus led the blind man out of the village (v. 23). It is part of the portrait of the earthly Jesus that in his great healings he seeks solitude, to be aside from the people; that distinguishes him from the Hellenistic miracle workers about whom many stories were bandied about. They sought sensation and the applause of the people; Jesus went apart from the people. What happened through his hands and words was also for him a wonderful event of God's closeness, and he guarded this secret of divine activity. This does not exclude that these deeds were intended as a testimony to the dawning time of salvation; they were intended to make people thoughtful and to lead them to faith. For that reason Jesus eschewed the multitude gaping with curiosity, and yet he did not withdraw from public activity.

The evangelist only gave stronger emphasis to this behavior of Jesus, and it is his interest in the *person of Jesus* which led him to do this. The healing actions of God which occurred through Jesus were also deeds of Jesus himself and testified to his being the Messiah and the Son of God. Jesus himself wanted to remain in obscurity, but his deeds could not be kept hidden. Mark wishes to make the faithful community more fully aware who this Jesus was: the true and unique One through whom God's salvation comes to man and in whom the great prophecies are fulfilled. But this Jesus can and will only be grasped in faith, and so he remains in a certain sense concealed. The people are seized by awe, they are beside themselves; but they do not really come to believe. That too is part of God's plan of salvation because Jesus must go the way of the cross (8:31) to give his life as a ransom for many (10:45).

The Second Meal Account (8:1-10)

¹In those days, when again a crowd had gathered, and they had nothing to eat, he called his disciples to him, and said to them, ²"I have compassion on the crowd, because they have been with me three days, and have nothing to eat; ³and if I send them away hungry to their homes, they will faint on the way; and some of them have come a long way." ⁴And his disciples answered him, "How can one feed these men with bread in the desert?" ⁵And he asked them, "How many loaves have you?" They said, "Seven." ⁶And he commanded the crowd to sit down on the ground; and he took the seven loaves, and having given thanks he broke them and gave them to his disciples to set before the people; and they set them before the crowd. ⁷And they had a few small fish; and having blessed them, he commanded that these also should be set before them. ⁸And they ate, and were satisfied; and they took up the broken pieces left over, seven baskets full. ⁹And there were about four thousand people. ¹⁰And he sent them away; and immediately he got into the boat with his disciples, and went to the district of Dalmanutha.

This account of a miraculous meal at which four thousand people were present was also found in the tradition by Mark, and he may well have taken it up into his gospel without

modification. He made no attempt to link this account with
the preceding stories. The story begins with the vague information, " in those days "; in the end the boat lands in the vicinity
of a place which bears the otherwise unknown and probably
corrupt name Dalmanutha. Perhaps the detail of 7:31 was
sufficient for Mark; he would then have imagined the event
to have taken place on the eastern shore of the sea, as in the
case of the first multiplication of loaves in 6:34-44. This lonely
region would certainly be a suitable stage for the event. If one
compares the whole story with the first meal account and one
rightly supposes that " Dalmanutha " is only a copyist's accidental distortion of " Magdala," the place of landing being the
plain of Gennesaret (cf. 6:53) as in the first meal, then a close
similarity between the two accounts is the result. Only the
numerical data differ; but here one cannot ask for exactness
considering the type and intention of the tradition. The conclusion suggests itself that we are concerned with two different
accounts of the same event. It cannot be doubted, however, that
Mark had two multiplications of bread in mind (cf. 8:19f.).

If we desire to pursue the intentions of the evangelist and
gain an understanding of him, we must think a little about this
problem which disquiets many Christians today because of the
question of the historicity of the tradition. The discrepancies
between other accounts of the synoptic gospels and between them
and John's gospel are so numerous and consequential that one
simply cannot classify the gospel writings as " writing history "
in our sense of the word. Our meditations on Mark's gospel
so far have shown clearly that, besides the historical interest,
the evangelist follows catechetical, didactic, and theological aims.
Especially in the account of the great miracle of the loaves in
the wilderness did these basic concerns, which guided him, come

to light. Why then should Mark, finding a second meal account
in the tradition, told similarly but not identically with somewhat
different numerical data, pass over this story in silence (as John
did)? Should he have checked whether it described the same
event? One could reply that he (as inspired author) should not
have transmitted something " false." On the other hand, one
must ask from a theological viewpoint what is the " truth "
which he wished to offer the readers of his gospel: an exact,
in all things " correct," stock-taking of historical occurrences,
or—based on history—the " truth " which believing readers ought
to know *for their salvation*. Surely the latter! Since the sup-
position of two multiplications of bread meets the greatest difficulties from an historical point of view, we will quietly assume
that the miraculous meal took place only once. Consequently,
we shall be free to take still greater notice of the theological
intentions of the gospel.

Since the time of the fathers of the church the opinion has
been held that the " second multiplication of bread " was for
Mark a sign of Jesus' pity for the pagans, as the first was such
for the people of Israel. The opinion is based on the " seven
baskets " outside the framework of this section (7:24, 31) and
they are interpreted symbolically. They were supposed to indicate
the seven functionaries of the Hellenistic section of the young
community at Jerusalem (Rev. 6) or the seven churches in the
address of the apocalypse (Rev. 1). But this is an arbitrary sup-
position; also, seven loaves are specified here by the disciples as
their provision (v. 5), in contrast with the five loaves and two
fish of the first account. These are discrepancies of the tradition
which have no significance for the miracle itself. More important
is the remark that some people had " come a long way " (v. 3).
In the adopted account, this and the fact that the crowd had

been with Jesus for three days (v. 2) were intended to establish
the compassion and solicitude of Jesus. Mark could have had
pagans in mind with those who came from afar—but he gives
no hint of this. Perhaps, as we have supposed in the case of
the deaf mute, his intention was to suggest to his pagan-Christian
readers to imagine among the crowd representatives of their
pagan world, without thereby denying the historical truth that
nothing of this is in the tradition. He transmits the story as he
found it and, at the same time, in his travel notes he offers a
glimpse for a pagan-Christian understanding: Jesus did not
exclude pagans from his compassion.

Otherwise, the story shows no special characteristics compared
with the first meal account, except that Jesus' *compassion with
the people* receives a stronger emphasis. On the other hand,
several details which gave the first account its historical background are absent: the scriptural quotation concerning the sheep
without a shepherd, the green grass, the reclining in groups of
a hundred and fifty. The story is told with greater simplicity,
more like a miracle of Jesus' compassion. On reading this pericope the community was to be moved by Jesus' kindness. To it
too Jesus continues to give the bread it needs for life, the
eucharistic bread. The " thanksgiving " over the bread and the
" blessing " over the fish, which are expressly recorded here,
could remind the community of its Lord's supper.

Although this account appears to be simpler and almost
poorer than the first, it was not superfluous for the evangelist
(quite apart from his concern for the pagans). For the disciples
this second meal, so Mark sees it, was intended as a new reinforced revelation of Jesus' Messiahship. They, who at a later
crossing of the sea are once again filled with external " bread
anxieties " (8:14–17), are now to grasp finally that there is more

at stake in Jesus' activity than the mere alleviation of earthly need. The two multiplications of bread were meant to open their eyes as to who Jesus was and what his intentions were. But they do not understand and have a hardened heart (vv. 17–21). In the scene which follows, the evangelist betrays what the bread miracles meant to him: a *self-revelation of Jesus*. In this the community is also admonished to produce that understanding in faith which the disciples lacked in those days. At her own meal celebrations the church is to recall the presence of her Lord who in divine compassion gives her the bread of life.

The Pharisees Demand a Sign (8 :11–13)

[11]The Pharisees came and began to argue with him, seeking from him a sign from heaven, to test him. [12]And he sighed deeply in his spirit, and said, " Why does this generation seek a sign? Truly, I say to you, no sign shall be given to this generation." [13]And he left them, and getting into the boat again he departed to the other side.

A completely different situation! Hardly has Jesus set foot on Jewish ground when the Pharisees, already known to the readers as enemies of Jesus (7 : 1, 5), approach him. They are now becoming more active; with full intention they come and demand that Jesus perform a " sign from heaven." They wish " to test him " and thereby bring about his downfall, since in their opinion he can and will not effect such a sign. Later, the same malicious intention gets more frequent mention (10 : 2; 12 : 15). The situation becomes more difficult and threatening for Jesus; the cross is already casting its shadow. But what do the Pharisees mean by their demand?

The Jews expect of a prophet that he bear witness to himself by a sign, a striking miracle. Indirectly, the Pharisees are acknowledging Jesus' special conduct, his teaching with " full authority," his daring decisions in law, but also his mighty works in healing and casting out demons. There is something unusual, prophetic, in his behavior. Yet they are doubtful that Jesus' power comes from God (cf. 3 : 22); God himself ought to acknowledge him and attest him by a " sign." This immediate attestation of God is what is meant by a " sign from heaven." If Jesus does not accomplish this, he is unmasked as a " false prophet." In reality it is merely their *unbelief* which is concealed behind this demand. It is precisely these deeds of healing which have already shown clearly that Jesus is the One sent by God, the bringer of salvation to the people. It is the blindness of unbelief that demands " signs " which have already been given, that does not recognize God's action which is hidden and yet cannot be ignored, and that challenges his miraculous power. Would these people believe if Jesus granted their desire for an extraordinary, spectacular miracle? Jesus never exposed himself to this deception and therefore always refused the demand for a miracle of attestation. Even the " sign of Jonas " (Lk. 11 : 29f.; Mt. 12 : 29f.) does not have this meaning. Jesus means here probably his coming at the parousia, when God will reveal and justify him like the prophet rescued from death. Then, however, it will be too late for conversion and faith; the requested miracle of attestation becomes a sign of judgment. If Jesus had given in to the demand of the Pharisees, he would have become unfaithful to his mission and his task to go the way of the obedient servant of God. For him this demand also involved a " temptation " which he, however, withstood (cf. 8 : 32f.).

Jesus " sighed " over " this generation " which seeks a sign.

A similar emotion takes hold of him as Mark has already recorded at the sabbath healing: anger and at the same time sadness at their hardness of heart (3:5). It is a sigh of pain at so much unbelief, but such obtuseness is characteristic of " this generation," by which Jesus means his contemporaries. It is the same *complaint and accusation* which he later articulates more clearly: "O faithless generation, how long am I to be with you? How long am I to bear with you?" (9:19). Then he gives the unbelieving challenger a decisive refusal, in the original text, combined with a declaration on oath: " Truly, I say to you, no sign shall be given to this generation." That is the severity with which all men of God have opposed human desires. Jesus remains firm in his demand for conversion and faith; he who does not believe the sign of salvation, who is seeking human assurance and challenges God, must bear the consequences of his unbelief (cf. 6:11). God cannot be constrained; *he* refuses to give such a sign. Then Jesus departs from these Pharisees, gets into the boat again, and moves away from them to the other side. And this withdrawal of his presence is already a judgment.

The Disciples' Failure to Understand (8:14–21)

[14]Now they had forgotten to bring bread; and they had only one loaf with them in the boat. [15]And he cautioned them, saying, " Take heed, beware of the leaven of the Pharisees and the leaven of Herod." [16]And they discussed it with one another, saying, " We have no bread." [17]And being aware of it, Jesus said to them, " Why do you discuss the fact that you have no bread? Do you not perceive and understand? Are your hearts

hardened? [18]*Having eyes do you not see, and having ears do*
you not hear? And do you not remember? [19]*When I broke the*
five loaves for five thousand, how many baskets full of broken
pieces did you take up?" They said to him, "Twelve." [20]*"And*
the seven for the four thousand, how many baskets full of broken
pieces did you take up?" And they said to him, "Seven."
[21]*And he said to them, "Do you not yet understand?"*

The simple and yet profound narrative skill of the oldest
evangelist comes to light with special efficacy in this conversation
during the crossing. One can suppose that Mark was confronted
with traditional material which gave an account of a crossing
of the sea and a "bread conversation" of Jesus with his disciples. This fits well into a section where bread and eating are
often referred to (6:35–44; 7:2, 5; 8:1–10). Mark, however, has
put this tradition into the service of his theological aims. Because
of the preceding story of the Pharisees' demand for a sign, he
inserts words of Jesus which originally probably stood in another
context and which almost interrupt this one: the warning
against the leaven of the Pharisees and of Herod (v. 15). Verse 16
would connect with verse 14 without an interruption and the
metaphor of the leaven remains obscure and ambiguous (cf. Lk.
16:12). However, the scene which Mark sketches in this fashion
remains very impressive: the disciples are so lost in everyday
worldly affairs that they take no heed of Jesus' serious warning
and continue to speak among themselves about their bread
worries. Here Jesus interrupts and speaks to them more re-
proachfully and adjuringly than ever before. Their thoughts are
so bound to worldly and external things that they do not understand the meaning of what they have experienced, the deep
significance of the multiplication of bread and the distinction of

the hour. They are in fact in that danger against which Jesus is warning them and are approaching that condition which normally characterizes the unbelieving outsider: *seeing but not perceiving, hearing but not understanding* (cf. 4:12). Their heart is hardened since the great meal (6:52); they have understood nothing of Jesus' Messianic ministry and also at the walk on the water they did not grasp the mystery of Jesus' person.

Even now Jesus does not disown his disciples but rather seeks to make them *see*. He reminds them of the miracle of the multiplication of bread, of the twelve baskets full of collected fragments and the seven baskets, which Mark does not forget in view of the second account. If, without verse 15, one could still think that with this reference to the multiplication of bread Jesus wanted to overcome the worldly worries of the disciples, this is entirely excluded by that weighty and serious admonition and by the urgent and sad warning against a hardness of heart. From the manner in which Mark contructs this bread-leaven conversation, every reader feels that here is an attitude at stake which concerns discipleship as such which threatens the spiritual existence of believers in its foundation. Jesus' question at the end reverberates for long afterwards: " Do you not yet understand?"

The warning against the leaven of the Pharisees and of Herod (v. 15) requires special attention. For the evangelist there still remains an echo of the unbelieving demand for a sign of which he had just given an account. Jesus seems still to be preoccupied with the attitude of the Pharisees, and for this the phrase about the leaven which the evangelist knew seemed suitable. Leaven was for the Jews a metaphor for an inner driving force, mostly in a bad sense; related to people, it signified the inclination to evil. Jesus' words, however, hardly refer to the inclination to morally wicked deeds in a narrower sense, to sin and vice; they refer rather to a corrupting *mentality* which fills people and can affect others by contagion.

Then Jesus also gives a warning against the leaven of Herod. As early as 3:6 the Pharisees are named together with the Herodians. There they held council with them as to how they could destroy Jesus. This ought not, however, lead us astray into thinking that the statement of Jesus about the leaven was intended to warn against external snares and murderous intentions. As formulated above, it refers rather to an inner corrupting mentality, and if Jesus warns his disciples against it, he means that they must not allow themselves to be infected by it. Herod himself has been introduced to the reader (6:14–29); in his judgment of Jesus he said mockingly that he must be the risen John the Baptist whom he had beheaded. That shows his cool, sceptical, unbelieving attitude towards Jesus. For him Jesus is at most interesting as a leader of a popular movement, as an extraordinary phenomenon; one must observe him for political reasons and when necessary render him harmless. The opinion has been expressed that the Pharisees and Herod were named together in the verse about the leaven because from a political viewpoint they were in a certain sense close to one another: they had in common, although for different reasons, their concern for the achievement of a united Jewish people and national state. Jesus, consequently, wanted to warn the disciples against nourishing in their hearts such political Messianic hopes. However, that is certainly too external an approach. Jesus is concerned with the inner human mentality, with the religious outlook. However, in their *unbelieving rejection* of Jesus the Pharisees and Herod were in agreement in spite of all differences. It is that unbelief which Jesus so startlingly came up against in the Pharisees' demand for a sign. Without testing his works and words, without allowing for the possibilities that God is at work here and that Jesus is doing God's business, they reject him. This is the blindness, the superficiality and intractability against which Jesus wants to warn his disciples also.

Mark would have understood the phrase in this way in this context. It is not surprising that Matthew and Luke give individual and divergent interpretations: Matthew relates the warning to the teaching of the Pharisees and the Sadducees (Mt. 6:12); Luke relates it to the " hypocrisy " of the Pharisees (Lk. 12:1), as concealment of one's own thoughts, an improbity and dishonesty, which someday will be revealed in any case (cf. Lk. 12:2f.). Mark detected the deepest reason for Jesus' warning: the imperviousness to God and his revelation which infects the hearts of such people.

Then the warning against the leaven of the Pharisees and of Herod corresponds to Jesus' reproachful and serious *admonition* addressed to the disciples (vv. 17–21). They are still uncomprehending. Even at Jesus' walk on the water the evangelist did not shrink from saying that " their hearts were hardened " (6:52). Jesus' penetrating questions addressed to his disciples at this new crossing are not merely rhetorical in intention; they have, in fact, not understood the meaning of the miracle of the loaves. Jesus does not want to imply that they have the " leaven " of the Pharisees already inside them, but he urgently warns them against it. At this hour when the attitude of the opponents is hardening and Jesus already sees approaching his fate of suffering ordained by God (cf. 8:31), he wants to preserve their faith from shipwreck.

The words about " not seeing and not hearing " must remind readers of that place in the parable chapter where Jesus had

characterized the attitude of "those outside" in similar terms
(4:12). To be sure, the wording here does not refer to the
Isaiah quotation (Is. 6:9f.), but to two other prophetic passages.
Jeremiah scolds the people: "O foolish and senseless people,
who have eyes but see not, who have ears but hear not" (Jer.
5:21). And Ezekiel speaks of a man in a "rebellious house,
who have eyes to see, but see not, who have ears to hear but
hear not" (Ezek. 12:2). Just as the old prophets had to execute
their mission among a foolish and rebellious people, the disciples
too are surrounded by a lack of understanding and unbelief and
are in grave danger of *conforming to their surroundings*. The
election of God, which has "given them the secret of God's
kingdom," is no proof against their own failure. So Jesus
reminds them of the revelation events which they have experienced at the meal (or meals) in the desert. They should open
their hearts and recognize with the eyes of faith that Jesus then
revealed himself as Messianic shepherd of the people and God's
bringer of salvation.

These very harsh words of Jesus which stand in contrast with
4:11f. (and which Matthew left out) cannot be explained only
in terms of the situation of the time under the burden of the
approaching passion of Jesus. The later situation of the community, to whom these words are also addressed, must be
considered. The inner state and disposition of the disciples is
also a *warning* for the believing readers. They too are surrounded by a lack of understanding and by unbelief; the
ignominious death of their master is a stumbling block or
folly (cf. 1 Cor. 1:23) for the unbelieving world. Human beings
continue to demand signs which are manifest and a gospel
which is humanly explicable. The disciples of Christ must look
deeper and grasp the way of the cross of their master as God's

counsel. Then it is necessary to be reminded of the divine revelations in the life of Jesus which were secret yet sufficiently manifest. Even the faithful Christians are not immune to a hardening of the heart which destroys their faith. The words of Jesus intend to warn them but also to stimulate them to a believing understanding. The miracle of the meal is perpetuated for them in the eucharistic meal which unites them with Christ, the risen and transfigured Lord.

The Healing of the Blind Man at Bethsaida (8 :22–26)

[22]*And they came to Bethsaida. And some people brought to him a blind man, and begged him to touch him.* [23]*And he took the blind man by the hand, and led him out of the village; and when he had spat on his eyes and laid his hands upon him, he asked him, " Do you see anything? "* [24]*And he looked up and said, " I see men; but they look like trees, walking."* [25]*Then again he laid his hands upon his eyes; and he looked intently and was restored, and saw everything clearly.* [26]*And he sent him away to his home, saying, " Do not even enter the village."*

This narrative of a healing is connected with the name of a place. Bethsaida lay to the east of the influx of the Jordan into the Sea of Galilee. The place is here called a " village," although it had been built up into a city by the Tetrarch Philippus (" Bethsaida Julias "). Perhaps the narrator was still thinking of the old fishing village. Other traits of the narrative strengthen the impression that it originates in a source characterized by archaic notions and found ready-made by Mark. The healing occurs through spittle and laying of hands on the eyes, two ancient means of healing in the popular view, and it occurs gradually. This indicates not only the seriousness of the case but also the exertion and pains of the healer. This ancient source has without bias recorded this, without taking into account that Jesus' healing powers might thereby be minimized. On the contrary, it was for this narrator rather a proof of the *great healing power of Jesus.* If the blind man has his sight restored gradually, at first seeing indistinctly men that "look like trees walking," and then, after repeated laying of hands and looking intently, seeing everything distinctly and clearly, then the hearers can participate in the miraculous process of how the blind man has his sight restored. Therefore, this narrator has the same objective in mind, that of depicting Jesus' extraordinary healing power, as the one who records only one word of command from Jesus. Mark records one more healing of a blind man, that of Bartimaeus in Jericho (10:46–52), and there Jesus says merely: "Go your way; your faith has made you well." The manner and intention of each narrator must be considered if one wishes to avoid false conclusions. Also in our story Jesus is not portrayed as a "magical healer"; the fact alone that he leads him out of the village and sends him home with the explicit command to avoid the village (and the people) contradicts this.

This is, therefore, an ancient story of healing which had no other aim but to depict the healing, and Mark has transmitted it unchanged. It is a parallel piece to the *healing of the deaf mute* (7:32–37) and very similar to it in the manner of narration. The introduction is almost the same: some people bring a man seriously afflicted to Jesus and beg him to lay his hands on him. In both cases Jesus takes the patient aside from the crowd and concerns himself about him with gestures of healing which the people of the time understood. In both cases Jesus uses spittle and uses his hands for the healing; he puts his finger into the ears of the deaf mute and lays his hands on the eyes of the blind man. Only the healing itself is described differently: in the case of the deaf mute Jesus utters a word of command; in the case of the blind man he omits it. Mark has introduced the first account with only a travel note (7:31) and added the command to silence and the remark that the people " proclaimed " the matter all the more. In this account at most only the last sentence, Jesus' instruction to the man to stay away from the village, originates from the evangelist. Perhaps originally there was a similar acclamation of the people here as in 7:37. It is in this way, therefore, that believing Christians, probably Jewish Christians, initially told the stories of Jesus' healings and saw in them the fulfillment of the ancient prophecies. This is also of value historically; one knew that thus Jesus worked and made the people marvel. But the intention of giving a completely accurate report was not always there.

Questioning the Disciples and Peter's Confession (8 :27–30)

[27]And Jesus went on with his disciples to the village of Caesarea Philippi; and on the way he asked his disciples, " Who do men say that I am?" [28]And they told him " John the Baptist; and others say Elijah; and others one of the prophets." [29]And he asked them, " But who do you say that I am?" Peter answered him, " You are the Messiah " [in the German version]. *[30]And he charged them to tell no one about him.*

To begin with Jesus asks his disciples who the people think he is. The question emerges almost of necessity from the portrayal so far, since the readers have frequently heard of the reaction of the people to the teaching and mighty works of Jesus but have never received satisfactory information concerning their attitude towards Jesus. For the most part the people are said to be " amazed " (1:27; 2:12), " astonished " (1:22; 6:2; 7:37), " overcome with amazement " (5:42), or they " marveled " (5:20). Only once (in an adopted account) do they speak more clearly about the fulfillment of the salvation prophecies (7:37). The reader is, however, not totally unprepared for the answer of the disciples. For after the mission of the twelve, in his account of Herod, the evangelist has specified the opinions of the people (6:14f.), and there it was clear that these opinions remained inadequate. The present answer of the disciples is almost identical with the opinions at the time. The opinions of the people have not changed, in spite of the great meal and the great healings which Mark narrates afterwards. The Galilean people cannot make *a clear judgment* and are incapable of arriving at a decisive profession of faith. In spite of all the admiration for the great benefactor and worker of miracles, they remain indecisive and vacillating. Thus Jesus does not comment on these popular opinions and now emphatically (" he himself ") asks his disciples: " But who do you say that I am?" Peter answered him clearly and unambiguously: " You are the Messiah."

Is that not the answer which Jesus has wished for? Does this not mean that the disciples, who up to now have been without understanding (8:17-21), have finally come to a full faith, or better: has not this knowledge been revealed to them, or at least to Peter, by God? We are so used to this idea from Matthew's version (16:16f.) that only with difficulty do we face the problem which our Mark text presents. Does Jesus joyfully accept Peter's confession? Why does he immediately charge his disciples to remain silent without in any way endorsing Peter's confession of the Messiah? And—still more confusing —how is it possible that the same Peter, a little later, tries to dissuade him from going his way of suffering (v. 32)? When one attempts to explain this revelation of Jesus' suffering, repugnant and incomprehensible as it was to Peter, one is astonished at the extraordinary severity of Jesus' reaction, repudiating him, who before has ostensibly made the highest confession of him, as a " Satan " who does not think God's thoughts but those of men (v. 33). Yet the quick succession of these two scenes must have a meaning for the evangelist. Is it really intended that Peter should be cast down from the highest heights of a confession inspired by God to the lowest depths of a temptation bearing Satan's imprint?

Therefore, it is understandable that not a few exegetes hold the extreme contrary view. They see in the Messiah confession of the leading disciple an answer which is in no way satisfactory to Jesus, the articulation of a *false expectation* which Jesus repudiates. They allege that Peter and the other disciples held the concept of a worldly-political kingdom of the Messiah which Jesus, from the beginning since the temptation of Satan in the desert, has rejected and most severely condemned. However, this explanation, which goes to the other extreme, has weighty objections against it. Could it be true that Peter and the circle of disciples disappointed Jesus more than the crowd? Why, then, does the transfiguration on the mountain (9: 7) not follow much later, for there God himself testifies to Jesus as his beloved Son in the presence of the three disciples, among them Peter. In the mind of the evangelist, is this scene not a confirmation of Peter's confession? The scene at Caesarea Philippi could not have had a totally negative meaning for Mark.

Perhaps another observation in Mark's gospel helps us in this embarrassment. In many places the evangelist reports that demons, whom Jesus intends to cast out, address him—certainly defensively—as the " Holy One of God " (1 : 24) or as the " Son of God " (3 : 11; 5 : 7). Jesus commands them not to make him known (3 : 12), surely for another reason than the command to silence imposed on the disciples. For the believing readers, however, these demonic confessions remain nonetheless significant. What these unclean spirits cry out for wicked reasons is nonetheless true: Jesus is the Son of God. Should not the confession of Peter also have the meaning of articulating their own confession for the *hearing community*? Of course, by the way Peter said it at the time, it is open to misunderstanding. Jesus has never—Mark knows this as well as the last evangelist John— called himself Messiah in the Jewish sense; for the Jews the " Messiah " was the theocratic king, the son of David (cf. 12 : 36f.) and Jesus did not intend to be an earthly liberator. It may be true that the disciples inclined towards such a misunderstanding (cf. 10 : 37) and that Peter was not free of this either. Nevertheless, his confession was not fully false, merely not yet clear and purified. In any case, he saw more in Jesus than the others in the crowd with their different opinions. So his confession, on the one hand, represents a climax and, on the other, it is not readily acceptable for Jesus and could even be dangerous if broadcast among the people. For that reason Jesus *forbids* the disciples to speak about him among the people, and after this he begins to reveal to the disciples his true Messiahship (in the Christian sense), the secret of the " Son of man " who by God's decree must suffer and die.

Matters are similar in the case of the solemn interrogation of Jesus by the high priest when he is asked about his Messiahship.

Jesus cannot simply answer " Yes," because he does not see himself as the promised liberator in the Jewish sense; nor can he answer " No," because he is the bringer of salvation promised by God but in a manner which does not correspond to Jewish expectations and transcends them in the highest degree. This true understanding of Jesus' Messiahship is disclosed in both cases by the title Son of man: the Son of man is the one who must first suffer and die (8:31), but will one day come raised up to God with the clouds of heaven (14:62). So the young church has understood her Lord and, in spite of the disputes about Jesus' original words, she has surely understood him aright.

When one looks at the scene of Caesarea Philippi from this point of view, there is no absolute contrast between Matthew and Mark. The oldest evangelist is more mindful of the historical conditions and cannot acknowledge the Messiah confession of Peter in all its dimensions. But he is aware of its significance for the church after Easter: then all misunderstanding is excluded and this profession receives its radiance in the light of the resurrection. From this standpoint Matthew looks back and discloses (as he did after the walk on the water, 14:33) the supra-temporal significance of Peter's confession; hence he consciously gives it a full Christian resonance: " You are the Messiah, the Son of the living God " (16:16).

But what does this scene mean for the Christian reader of Mark's gospel? No less than that, at the *end* of the Galilean ministry of Jesus, their *confession of Jesus* as the promised Messiah is attested through the mouth of the leading disciple. That was the hidden significance of his ministry among the people of Israel as it was portrayed in all the chapters that went before. At the same time, however, they are made aware of how difficult and ambiguous this confession was in the situation of that time. Jesus was, in his behavior and aims, quite different from what the Jews imagined their Messiah would be. For that reason, in spite of all admiration, he found no true faith among the people and concluded the great Galilean ministry a failure on the outside. Thus his human opponents could rise up against him and he had to go the way of the cross. His death, however, was, according to God's plan, intended for the salvation of all who believe in the crucified and risen Messiah, for Jews as well as pagans. Peter's Messiah profession still needed clarification and explanation, and above all did the revelation of the mystery of suffering. It needed also to mature to the deepest knowledge, which certainly is already accessible to believing eyes observing the earthly ministry of Jesus, but becomes certainty only after the resurrection of Jesus: this Messiah is truly God's Son.